D0685798

the second book of moses, called

exodus

authorised king james version

printed by authority

published by canongate

with an introduction by | david grossman

First published in Great Britain in 1998
by Canongate Books Ltd
14 High Street, Edinburgh EH1 1TE

10 9 8 7 6 5 4 3 2

Introduction copyright © David Grossman 1998
Translation of introduction copyright © Marsha Weinstein 1998
The moral right of the author has been asserted

British Library Cataloguing-in-Publication Data
A catalogue record is available on request from
the British Library

ISBN 0 86241 790 2

Typeset by Palimpsest Book Production
Book design by Paddy Cramsie
Printed and bound in Great Britain
by Caledonian International, Bishopbriggs

LICENCE: *In terms of the Letters Patent granted by Her late Majesty Queen
Victoria to Her Printers for Scotland and of the Instructions issued by Her said
Majesty in Council, dated Eleventh July Eighteen Hundred and Thirty nine, I hereby
License and Authorise Canongate Books Limited, Fourteen High Street, Edinburgh,
to Print and Publish, as by the Authority of Her Majesty Queen Elizabeth the Second,
but so far as regards the Text of the Authorised Version only, an Edition of the Book
of Exodus in Palatino Type as proposed in their Declaration dated the Twenty first
day of May Nineteen Hundred and Ninety eight.*

Dated at London the Twenty eighth day of July Nineteen Hundred and Ninety eight.

HARDIE, Lord Advocate

a note about pocket canons

The Authorised King James Version of the Bible, translated between 1603–11, coincided with an extraordinary flowering of English literature. This version, more than any other, and possibly more than any other work in history, has had an influence in shaping the language we speak and write today. Presenting individual books from the Bible as separate volumes, as they were originally conceived, encourages the reader to approach them as literary works in their own right.

The first twelve books in this series encompass categories as diverse as history, fiction, philosophy, love poetry and law. Each Pocket Canon also has its own introduction, specially commissioned from an impressive range of writers, which provides a personal interpretation of the text and explores its contemporary relevance.

David Grossman is one of Israel's leading writers. He is author of four award-winning and internationally acclaimed novels including See Under: Love, The Smile of the Lamb, The Book of Intimate Grammar *and* The Zigzag Kid. *He has also writtten two powerful journalistic accounts about his encounters with Palestinians,* The Yellow Wind *and* Sleeping on a Wire, *as well as a number of children's books and a play. He was born in Jerusalem, where he now lives with his wife and three children.*

introduction by david grossman

Into the swirl of events at the beginning *The Book of Exodus* – the tale of the bondage and oppression of the children of Israel and the growing enmity between the Israelites and Egyptians – seeps another, more personal and poignant story: a Hebrew child is born and his mother, who would save him from the death decreed for all sons by Pharaoh, lays him in a basket of bulrushes and sets the basket in the Nile. There, among the reeds, the daughter of the King of Egypt finds him. Pharaoh's daughter knows instantly that he is 'one of the Hebrews' children', but nevertheless decides to raise him as her son; she is the one who gives him his name, Moses.

How enchanting the entwining of this winsome tale with the tempestuous, epic myth of the birth of a nation. In a sense, this is the fabric of the entire book, an almost illusive weaving of fairy tale with strict legal and religious code: the warp – rods that turn into serpents, a vicious, cruel king, a land blighted by a plague of frogs; the woof – the giving of the law on Mount Sinai, the moment at which a people becomes welded to its destiny.

Reading *The Book of Exodus* is charged with tension: between the miserable, 'childlike' state of the children of

Israel, a people physically and spiritually enslaved, and the exalted role God has chosen for them, heedless of the pace of their spiritual and moral development. Perhaps this is the truly demanding journey made by the children of Israel in *The Book of Exodus*: from clan to nation, from slavery to freedom.

II

Here in my study in Jerusalem, in Israel, in 'the promised land' to which the Jews have returned time and again from exile, I think about my forefathers, the children of Israel, during those first days after the maelstrom that uprooted them from Egypt. They are in the desert, and the desert is empty. They are being led, like an immense herd, to an unknown destination. What can they cling to? They escaped bondage in Egypt, but also abandoned their daily routine, their habits and customs, a familiar place and the social interactions and hierarchies that had become fixed over the course of generations. Suddenly everything is new and strange. Nothing can be taken for granted. What had appeared to be the end of the road, now appears to be its beginning. Somewhere in the heavens hovers the spirit of a God who seems to be benevolent; yet they, who have seen how He dealt with the Egyptians, know how unpredictable, brutal and fierce He can be.

Stunned, they stride onward, as if in a void. They follow their leader, a man who never lived among them, who from the time he was weaned lived in the king's palace and then in Midian. He tells them they are at long last free men, but perhaps free is the last thing they feel or want to be. Every day brings new experiences, new religious regulations and laws, and strange food – enough for one day – that falls from the skies.

If they have any spirit left they will realize that a miracle has befallen them, that they are privileged to have been given the chance to reinvent themselves, to be redeemed. If they dare, they can fashion a new identity for themselves. But to do so they must fight the ponderous gravity of habit, of anxiety and doubt, of inner bondage.

Maybe their hearts swelled at times – the expansive, dramatic landscapes of Sinai could have awakened unfamiliar feelings in the hearts of those who had for generations lived the choked lives of slaves in the confines of huts. Suddenly the body could try broader, more daring movements. Perhaps an ancient memory, thousands of years old, flickered, of their forefathers' wending their way toward Egypt across this very desert on a journey of which only shards of legend remain. Perhaps their carrying the body of Joseph, son of Jacob, to burial in the land of Israel made tangible for them the abstract promise of return to their country; return to the place where Joseph was a child, and Jacob before him lived; return home.

In addition, a new factor entered their lives: calendar time. God determined the cycle of their days, sealing the week with the Sabbath (*Exodus* 16:23). Since the six days of creation this concept of the 'week' had hovered over the

Torah, yet only now does it become clear to the reader that this concept was apparently known to God alone. Now He imparts it to His people. Can we, who were born within calendar time, fathom the impact this conceptual change must have had on human beings? Did it strengthen their sense of the circular, the cyclical, the monotonous? Or did time suddenly seem to be just another dimension of the desert in which they were trapped?

Not only did God create the 'circle of the week', but He designated holidays and festivals, setting the new year at Passover to emphasize its historic, religious and national significance. What did the children of Israel feel about God's having inscribed them in the historical consciousness of generations to come, while they themselves were but the dust of men, bewildered and frightened? Did they know they were only one step on the road to another, more exalted existence? At the end of a long day's wandering, as they sat by a dying fire, did a bitter, tragic silence fall as they realized, vaguely, that they were but putty in God's hands, their tortured existence destined to become a 'history' and a religion, an 'epic' tale, and their ability to comprehend this tale no more than that of letters to comprehend a book?

III

In *The Book of Numbers* (14:18 ff), God decrees that the entire generation of those who fled Egypt – a defiant generation that consistently refused to believe in God wholeheartedly and with complete faith – will be destroyed in the desert and not brought into the promised land. Yet the *Zohar*[1] calls this generation the 'generation of knowledge'; some envy its having witnessed God's wondrous acts during the exodus from Egypt, and its presence at the giving of the law on Mount Sinai. Nevertheless, throughout their history the Jewish people have conceived of the 'desert generation' as a lost, transitional generation, rootless and lacking identity and faith, a generation tossed in the 'chasm' between past and future, consumed by anxiety regarding its destiny. According to ancient Jewish legend, on the eve of *Tisha B'Av*[2] during the sojourn in the desert, the children of Israel would dig themselves graves and lie in them, rising in the morning to see who had remained alive.

Even today, the Jewish people read in the Passover *Haggadah* that 'in every generation, each individual is bound to regard himself as if he personally had gone forth from Egypt'. This is a direct summons to the people of Israel to examine the essential components of their identity.

It is difficult to grasp just how crucial those forty years in the desert were to the formation of the Jewish people as a people. During those years, the lines of its 'national character' were drawn through the crucible of slavery and 'victimhood'

---

[1] A commentary on the *Five Books of Moses*, the *Zohar* is a fundamental work of Judaism's mystic teachings (trans.).
[2] The ninth day of the Hebrew month of *Av* is observed by fasting, prayer and mourning in commemoration of the destruction of the first and second Temples, and other calamities that have befallen the Jewish people on that date (trans.).

and the ensuing phenomenal propensity for redemption and rejuvenation. Moreover, a complex pattern of contradictory emotions was formed: pride, indeed arrogance, over being 'the chosen people', tempered by a sense of having been banished, even cursed – the price of such mysterious chosenness; comfort and security in the knowledge of being the people of Yahweh, tempered by a fear of that same invisible and fickle God, Himself seemingly buffeted by internal storms rife with contradiction; and a taste for wandering, branded on the consciousness during the wandering in the desert, tempered by an intense longing for a 'promised land' where – and only where – existence could at last be merged with identity, and a zest for living could be freed.

Wandering is also searching, and longing always gives rise to new ideas and abstract thought. Gradually, searching and longing affect the dormant consciousness of this people that for generations had been subjugated, tethered to physical distress and hardship, become ossified. Searching and longing leave a unique mark on this people, reflected in its ideological motivation, its penchant for the abstract and talent at keeping an entire reality alive in its imagination, its aspirations and yearnings and, above all, its ability to be revitalized by the power of a dream, to use a dream to rise above real affliction.

IV

The people of Israel was formed as a result of a commandment to wander to a new place. God said to our forefather

Abraham, 'Get thee out of thy country, and from thy kindred, and from thy father's house, unto a land that I will show thee' (*Genesis* 12:1). While at that time many tribes and peoples wandered constantly in search of sustenance, such wandering was never an end in itself – a national end in itself – as it was for the Jewish people, and as it is presented in the Books of *Genesis* and *Exodus*.

In retrospect, it seems that during those years in the desert these two contradictory elements – the urge to wander and the longing for a 'place' – became forces so integral to the soul of the Jewish people that it is difficult to know which is stronger. Perhaps this is one reason why for centuries the people of Israel have been mired in the same dilemma, lacking a sense of inner conviction: are they a people of place, or a people of time? That is, can the people of Israel live in a country with traceable, permanent borders and a distinctly national (or any other) 'character', or are they doomed, inherently, to seek out a 'borderless' existence of perpetual movement, of alternate exile and return, assimilation and individuation, restoration and change generation after generation, forever eluding definition and vulnerable to surrounding forces that would fortify or destroy them by turn?

Perhaps this also explains why for centuries other peoples have been so eager to determine just what a 'Jew' is, hemming him in to some 'definition' or other based on distinct characteristics, confining his fields of commerce or even penning him into a ghetto, as if to make him comprehensible, easy to monitor.

After all, this is also a description of the utter, onerous foreignness of one people among many. Indeed, from the harsh and violent exodus from Egypt to God's insistence on the separateness of this people and His exclusive 'possession' of it, *The Book of Exodus* brings into sharp relief the unique status of the Jewish people: its ability to quickly uproot itself, as if cutting itself out along an ever-present dotted line, coupled with a trenchant need to mingle with others, to become lost in them and thereby, paradoxically, to distill its identity, to define itself for itself.

This may further explain the necessity to the Jewish people of spending those forty years in the desert, almost completely cut off from other peoples and identities. Those years served as a lengthy cocoon stage, the final one before the Jewish people was hatched into its history, giving it time to formulate its identity solely through internal dialogue and an acceptance of its essential components, through countless occurrences, crises and climaxes.

V

More than any other of the *Five Books of Moses*, *The Book of Exodus* lays the foundation for the sense of 'epic', of myth, that has dogged the Jewish people since the exodus from Egypt, until the present. This is a most complex, disturbing feeling; perhaps it has contributed to Jewish existence having become, in the eyes of other peoples, an immense 'drama' – too immense – that cannot be confronted without being turned into a symbol or metaphor for something else.

In other words, that existence is never just an existence, the Jews never just a people among peoples. This attitude is so entrenched, so ancient that it is difficult to know whether it resulted from the historic fate of the Jews or was 'projected' onto them and determined their fate. It burdens the 'Jew' by ascribing him either a heavy load of sentimental ideals or a refutably demonic character. The Jew is stretched between these two extremes, suffering from them, of course, but also surely finding solace in the equally ancient sense that his suffering and wandering has 'meaning', that a hidden author's intent will at some point lend the whole story significance.

It is no less interesting to ponder the extent to which the Israelis of today, citizens of a sovereign, free, strong Israel, are impaired by a perception of themselves as a 'symbol' of something else – one they may not really, truly want to give up. To what extent does this warped self-perception cause them to fall short of their aspiration to be at long last a people living in its country, a people that has fully internalized its sovereignty and might, and that is capable of conducting a life of minutiae, of concessions, of practical compromises with its neighbours, a normal people, a people like any other?

As one who was born in Israel and has lived there all his life, I read *The Book of Exodus* and wonder how it is that even today, and even by its inhabitants, Israel is still called 'the promised land'. That is, not 'the land that was promised' or 'a land of promise', but the land that is still promised, and that, even after the return to Zion, has not yet been fulfilled, and whose people have not yet fully realized their potential. It would seem that the disenfranchisement of the 'desert generation' still casts its spell within Israel, fifty years after the State's establishment.

This 'eternal promise' carries with it the hope of growth and a potential for almost limitless freedom of thought, and flexibility of perspective, regarding things that have become fossilized in their definitions. However, it is inevitably tainted by the 'curse of the eternal', a latent, deep-seated sense of inability to ever achieve fulfilment, and a concomitant inability to address fundamental questions of identity, of belonging to a place or of that place's permanent borders, vis à vis its neighbours.

This may be the principal anomaly of the Jewish people's identity, in Israel as in the diaspora. It may be the secret of that people's endurance and vitality, but it doubtless also makes it constantly vulnerable to tragedy in a world that is all definitions and borders. *The Book of Exodus,* the grand story of the childhood of the Jewish people, sketches the primordial face of that people as it is being formed and, as we now know, describes what will be its fate throughout thousands of years of history.

Translated from the Hebrew by Marsha Weinstein

the second book of moses, called exodus

Now these are the names of the children of Israel, which came into Egypt; every man and his household came with Jacob: ²Reuben, Simeon, Levi, and Judah, ³Issachar, Zebulun, and Benjamin, ⁴Dan, and Naphtali, Gad, and Asher. ⁵And all the souls that came out of the loins of Jacob were seventy souls, for Joseph was in Egypt already. ⁶And Joseph died, and all his brethren, and all that generation.

⁷And the children of Israel were fruitful, and increased abundantly, and multiplied, and waxed exceeding mighty, and the land was filled with them. ⁸Now there arose up a new king over Egypt, which knew not Joseph. ⁹And he said unto his people, 'Behold, the people of the children of Israel are more and mightier than we. ¹⁰Come on, let us deal wisely with them, lest they multiply, and it come to pass, that, when there falleth out any war, they join also unto our enemies, and fight against us, and so get them up out of the land.' ¹¹Therefore they did set over them taskmasters to afflict them with their burdens. And they built for Pharaoh treasure cities, Pithom and Raamses. ¹²But the more they afflicted them, the more they multiplied and grew. And they were grieved because of the children of Israel. ¹³And the Egyptians made the children of Israel to serve with rigour, ¹⁴and they

made their lives bitter with hard bondage, in morter, and in brick, and in all manner of service in the field. All their service, wherein they made them serve, was with rigour.

¹⁵And the king of Egypt spake to the Hebrew midwives, of which the name of the one was Shiphrah, and the name of the other Puah, ¹⁶and he said, 'When ye do the office of a midwife to the Hebrew women, and see them upon the stools; if it be a son, then ye shall kill him: but if it be a daughter, then she shall live.' ¹⁷But the midwives feared God, and did not as the king of Egypt commanded them, but saved the men children alive. ¹⁸And the king of Egypt called for the midwives, and said unto them, 'Why have ye done this thing, and have saved the men children alive?' ¹⁹And the midwives said unto Pharaoh, 'Because the Hebrew women are not as the Egyptian women; for they are lively, and are delivered ere the midwives come in unto them.' ²⁰Therefore God dealt well with the midwives: and the people multiplied, and waxed very mighty. ²¹And it came to pass, because the midwives feared God, that he made them houses. ²²And Pharaoh charged all his people, saying, 'Every son that is born ye shall cast into the river, and every daughter ye shall save alive.'

2 And there went a man of the house of Levi, and took to wife a daughter of Levi. ²And the woman conceived, and bare a son: and when she saw him that he was a goodly child, she hid him three months. ³And when she could not longer hide him, she took for him an ark of bulrushes, and daubed it with slime and with pitch, and put the child

therein; and she laid it in the flags by the river's brink. ⁴And his sister stood afar off, to wit what would be done to him.

⁵And the daughter of Pharaoh came down to wash herself at the river; and her maidens walked along by the river's side; and when she saw the ark among the flags, she sent her maid to fetch it. ⁶And when she had opened it, she saw the child; and, behold, the babe wept. And she had compassion on him, and said, 'This is one of the Hebrews' children.' ⁷Then said his sister to Pharaoh's daughter, 'Shall I go and call to thee a nurse of the Hebrew women, that she may nurse the child for thee?' ⁸And Pharaoh's daughter said to her, 'Go.' And the maid went and called the child's mother. ⁹And Pharaoh's daughter said unto her, 'Take this child away, and nurse it for me, and I will give thee thy wages.' And the woman took the child, and nursed it. ¹⁰And the child grew, and she brought him unto Pharaoh's daughter, and he became her son. And she called his name Moses: and she said, 'Because I drew him out of the water.'

¹¹And it came to pass in those days, when Moses was grown, that he went out unto his brethren, and looked on their burdens, and he spied an Egyptian smiting an Hebrew, one of his brethren. ¹²And he looked this way and that way, and when he saw that there was no man, he slew the Egyptian, and hid him in the sand. ¹³And when he went out the second day, behold, two men of the Hebrews strove together, and he said to him that did the wrong, 'Wherefore smitest thou thy fellow?' ¹⁴And he said, 'Who made thee a prince and a judge over us? Intendest thou to kill me, as thou killedst the

Egyptian?' And Moses feared, and said, 'Surely this thing is known.' ¹⁵ Now when Pharaoh heard this thing, he sought to slay Moses. But Moses fled from the face of Pharaoh, and dwelt in the land of Midian; and he sat down by a well. ¹⁶ Now the priest of Midian had seven daughters, and they came and drew water, and filled the troughs to water their father's flock. ¹⁷ And the shepherds came and drove them away, but Moses stood up and helped them, and watered their flock. ¹⁸ And when they came to Reuel their father, he said, 'How is it that ye are come so soon today?' ¹⁹ And they said, 'An Egyptian delivered us out of the hand of the shepherds, and also drew water enough for us, and watered the flock.' ²⁰ And he said unto his daughters, 'And where is he? Why is it that ye have left the man? Call him, that he may eat bread.' ²¹ And Moses was content to dwell with the man, and he gave Moses Zipporah his daughter. ²² And she bare him a son, and he called his name Gershom, for he said, 'I have been a stranger in a strange land.'

²³ And it came to pass in process of time, that the king of Egypt died, and the children of Israel sighed by reason of the bondage, and they cried, and their cry came up unto God by reason of the bondage. ²⁴ And God heard their groaning, and God remembered his covenant with Abraham, with Isaac, and with Jacob. ²⁵ And God looked upon the children of Israel, and God had respect unto them.

3 Now Moses kept the flock of Jethro his father-in-law, the priest of Midian; and he led the flock to the backside

of the desert, and came to the mountain of God, even to Horeb. ²And the angel of the Lord appeared unto him in a flame of fire out of the midst of a bush, and he looked, and, behold, the bush burned with fire, and the bush was not consumed. ³And Moses said, 'I will now turn aside, and see this great sight, why the bush is not burnt.' ⁴And when the Lord saw that he turned aside to see, God called unto him out of the midst of the bush, and said, 'Moses, Moses.' And he said, 'Here am I.' ⁵And he said, 'Draw not nigh hither: put off thy shoes from off thy feet, for the place whereon thou standest is holy ground.' ⁶Moreover he said, 'I am the God of thy father, the God of Abraham, the God of Isaac, and the God of Jacob.' And Moses hid his face, for he was afraid to look upon God.

⁷And the Lord said, 'I have surely seen the affliction of my people which are in Egypt, and have heard their cry by reason of their taskmasters, for I know their sorrows; ⁸and I am come down to deliver them out of the hand of the Egyptians, and to bring them up out of that land unto a good land and a large, unto a land flowing with milk and honey; unto the place of the Canaanites, and the Hittites, and the Amorites, and the Perizzites, and the Hivites, and the Jebusites. ⁹Now therefore, behold, the cry of the children of Israel is come unto me, and I have also seen the oppression wherewith the Egyptians oppress them. ¹⁰Come now therefore, and I will send thee unto Pharaoh, that thou mayest bring forth my people the children of Israel out of Egypt.'

¹¹And Moses said unto God, 'Who am I, that I should go

unto Pharaoh, and that I should bring forth the children of Israel out of Egypt?' ¹²And he said, 'Certainly I will be with thee; and this shall be a token unto thee, that I have sent thee: when thou hast brought forth the people out of Egypt, ye shall serve God upon this mountain. ¹³And Moses said unto God, 'Behold, when I come unto the children of Israel, and shall say unto them, "The God of your fathers hath sent me unto you," and they shall say to me, "What is his name?" what shall I say unto them?' ¹⁴And God said unto Moses, 'I am that I am,' and he said, 'Thus shalt thou say unto the children of Israel, "'I am' hath sent me unto you."' ¹⁵And God said moreover unto Moses, 'Thus shalt thou say unto the children of Israel, "The Lord God of your fathers, the God of Abraham, the God of Isaac, and the God of Jacob, hath sent me unto you." This is my name for ever, and this is my memorial unto all generations. ¹⁶Go, and gather the elders of Israel together, and say unto them, "The Lord God of your fathers, the God of Abraham, of Isaac, and of Jacob, appeared unto me, saying, 'I have surely visited you, and seen that which is done to you in Egypt. ¹⁷And I have said I will bring you up out of the affliction of Egypt unto the land of the Canaanites, and the Hittites, and the Amorites, and the Perizzites, and the Hivites, and the Jebusites, unto a land flowing with milk and honey.'" ¹⁸And they shall hearken to thy voice; and thou shalt come, thou and the elders of Israel, unto the king of Egypt, and ye shall say unto him, "The Lord God of the Hebrews hath met with us; and now let us go, we beseech thee, three days' journey into the wilderness, that we may sacrifice to the Lord our God."

¹⁹'And I am sure that the king of Egypt will not let you go, no, not by a mighty hand. ²⁰And I will stretch out my hand, and smite Egypt with all my wonders which I will do in the midst thereof, and after that he will let you go. ²¹And I will give this people favour in the sight of the Egyptians; and it shall come to pass, that, when ye go, ye shall not go empty. ²²But every woman shall borrow of her neighbour, and of her that sojourneth in her house, jewels of silver, and jewels of gold, and raiment; and ye shall put them upon your sons, and upon your daughters; and ye shall spoil the Egyptians.'

4 And Moses answered and said, 'But, behold, they will not believe me, nor hearken unto my voice, for they will say, "The Lord hath not appeared unto thee."' ²And the Lord said unto him, 'What is that in thine hand?' And he said, 'A rod.' ³And he said, 'Cast it on the ground.' And he cast it on the ground, and it became a serpent; and Moses fled from before it. ⁴And the Lord said unto Moses, 'Put forth thine hand, and take it by the tail,' and he put forth his hand, and caught it, and it became a rod in his hand: ⁵'that they may believe that the Lord God of their fathers, the God of Abraham, the God of Isaac, and the God of Jacob, hath appeared unto thee.'

⁶And the Lord said furthermore unto him, 'Put now thine hand into thy bosom.' And he put his hand into his bosom, and when he took it out, behold, his hand was leprous as snow. ⁷And he said, 'Put thine hand into thy bosom again.' And he put his hand into his bosom again, and plucked it

out of his bosom, and, behold, it was turned again as his other flesh. ⁸'And it shall come to pass, if they will not believe thee, neither hearken to the voice of the first sign, that they will believe the voice of the latter sign. ⁹And it shall come to pass, if they will not believe also these two signs, neither hearken unto thy voice, that thou shalt take of the water of the river, and pour it upon the dry land; and the water which thou takest out of the river shall become blood upon the dry land.'

¹⁰And Moses said unto the Lord, 'O my Lord, I am not eloquent, neither heretofore, nor since thou hast spoken unto thy servant: but I am slow of speech, and of a slow tongue.' ¹¹And the Lord said unto him, 'Who hath made man's mouth? Or who maketh the dumb, or deaf, or the seeing, or the blind? Have not I the Lord? ¹²Now therefore go, and I will be with thy mouth, and teach thee what thou shalt say.' ¹³And he said, 'O my Lord, send, I pray thee, by the hand of him whom thou wilt send.' ¹⁴And the anger of the Lord was kindled against Moses, and he said, 'Is not Aaron the Levite thy brother? I know that he can speak well. And also, behold, he cometh forth to meet thee: and when he seeth thee, he will be glad in his heart. ¹⁵And thou shalt speak unto him, and put words in his mouth; and I will be with thy mouth, and with his mouth, and will teach you what ye shall do. ¹⁶And he shall be thy spokesman unto the people; and he shall be, even he shall be to thee instead of a mouth, and thou shalt be to him instead of God. ¹⁷And thou shalt take this rod in thine hand, wherewith thou shalt do signs.'

¹⁸And Moses went and returned to Jethro his father-in-law, and said unto him, 'Let me go, I pray thee, and return unto my brethren which are in Egypt, and see whether they be yet alive.' And Jethro said to Moses, 'Go in peace.' ¹⁹And the Lord said unto Moses in Midian, 'Go, return into Egypt: for all the men are dead which sought thy life.' ²⁰And Moses took his wife and his sons, and set them upon an ass, and he returned to the land of Egypt, and Moses took the rod of God in his hand. ²¹And the Lord said unto Moses, 'When thou goest to return into Egypt, see that thou do all those wonders before Pharaoh, which I have put in thine hand: but I will harden his heart, that he shall not let the people go. ²²And thou shalt say unto Pharaoh, "Thus saith the Lord, 'Israel is my son, even my firstborn. ²³And I say unto thee, let my son go, that he may serve me, and if thou refuse to let him go, behold, I will slay thy son, even thy firstborn.'"'

²⁴And it came to pass by the way in the inn, that the Lord met him, and sought to kill him. ²⁵Then Zipporah took a sharp stone, and cut off the foreskin of her son, and cast it at his feet, and said, 'Surely a bloody husband art thou to me.' ²⁶So he let him go: then she said, 'A bloody husband thou art, because of the circumcision.'

²⁷And the Lord said to Aaron, 'Go into the wilderness to meet Moses.' And he went, and met him in the mount of God, and kissed him. ²⁸And Moses told Aaron all the words of the Lord who had sent him, and all the signs which he had commanded him.

²⁹And Moses and Aaron went and gathered together all

the elders of the children of Israel, ³⁰ and Aaron spake all the words which the Lord had spoken unto Moses, and did the signs in the sight of the people. ³¹And the people believed; and when they heard that the Lord had visited the children of Israel, and that he had looked upon their affliction, then they bowed their heads and worshipped.

5 And afterward Moses and Aaron went in, and told Pharaoh, 'Thus saith the Lord God of Israel, "Let my people go, that they may hold a feast unto me in the wilderness."' ²And Pharaoh said, 'Who is the Lord, that I should obey his voice to let Israel go? I know not the Lord, neither will I let Israel go.' ³And they said, 'The God of the Hebrews hath met with us: let us go, we pray thee, three days' journey into the desert, and sacrifice unto the Lord our God; lest he fall upon us with pestilence, or with the sword.' ⁴And the king of Egypt said unto them, 'Wherefore do ye, Moses and Aaron, let the people from their works? Get you unto your burdens.' ⁵And Pharaoh said, 'Behold, the people of the land now are many, and ye make them rest from their burdens.' ⁶And Pharaoh commanded the same day the taskmasters of the people, and their officers, saying, ⁷'Ye shall no more give the people straw to make brick, as heretofore; let them go and gather straw for themselves. ⁸And the tale of the bricks, which they did make heretofore, ye shall lay upon them; ye shall not diminish ought thereof, for they be idle; therefore they cry, saying, "Let us go and sacrifice to our God." ⁹Let there more work be laid upon the men, that they may labour

therein; and let them not regard vain words.'

¹⁰And the taskmasters of the people went out, and their officers, and they spake to the people, saying, 'Thus saith Pharaoh, "I will not give you straw. ¹¹Go ye, get you straw where ye can find it; yet not ought of your work shall be diminished."' ¹²So the people were scattered abroad throughout all the land of Egypt to gather stubble instead of straw. ¹³And the taskmasters hasted them, saying, 'Fulfil your works, your daily tasks, as when there was straw.' ¹⁴And the officers of the children of Israel, which Pharaoh's taskmasters had set over them, were beaten, and demanded, 'Wherefore have ye not fulfilled your task in making brick both yesterday and to day, as heretofore?'

¹⁵Then the officers of the children of Israel came and cried unto Pharaoh, saying, 'Wherefore dealest thou thus with thy servants? ¹⁶There is no straw given unto thy servants, and they say to us, "Make brick," and, behold, thy servants are beaten; but the fault is in thine own people.' ¹⁷But he said, 'Ye are idle, ye are idle; therefore ye say, "Let us go and do sacrifice to the Lord." ¹⁸Go therefore now, and work; for there shall no straw be given you, yet shall ye deliver the tale of bricks.' ¹⁹And the officers of the children of Israel did see that they were in evil case, after it was said, 'Ye shall not minish ought from your bricks of your daily task.'

²⁰And they met Moses and Aaron, who stood in the way, as they came forth from Pharaoh, ²¹and they said unto them, 'The Lord look upon you, and judge; because ye have made our savour to be abhorred in the eyes of Pharaoh, and in the

eyes of his servants, to put a sword in their hand to slay us.'
²²And Moses returned unto the Lord, and said, 'Lord, wherefore hast thou so evil entreated this people? Why is it that
thou hast sent me? ²³ For since I came to Pharaoh to speak in
thy name, he hath done evil to this people; neither hast thou
delivered thy people at all.'

6 Then the Lord said unto Moses, 'Now shalt thou see
what I will do to Pharaoh, for with a strong hand shall
he let them go, and with a strong hand shall he drive them
out of his land.' ²And God spake unto Moses, and said unto
him, 'I am the Lord, ³and I appeared unto Abraham, unto
Isaac, and unto Jacob, by the name of God Almighty, but by
my name "Jehovah" was I not known to them. ⁴And I have
also established my covenant with them, to give them the
land of Canaan, the land of their pilgrimage, wherein they
were strangers. ⁵And I have also heard the groaning of the
children of Israel, whom the Egyptians keep in bondage;
and I have remembered my covenant. ⁶ Wherefore say unto
the children of Israel, "I am the Lord, and I will bring you
out from under the burdens of the Egyptians, and I will rid
you out of their bondage, and I will redeem you with a stretched out arm, and with great judgments. ⁷And I will take
you to me for a people, and I will be to you a God, and ye
shall know that I am the Lord your God, which bringeth you
out from under the burdens of the Egyptians. ⁸And I will
bring you in unto the land, concerning the which I did swear
to give it to Abraham, to Isaac, and to Jacob; and I will give it

you for an heritage. I am the Lord."'

⁹And Moses spake so unto the children of Israel, but they hearkened not unto Moses for anguish of spirit, and for cruel bondage. ¹⁰And the Lord spake unto Moses, saying, ¹¹'Go in, speak unto Pharaoh king of Egypt, that he let the children of Israel go out of his land.' ¹²And Moses spake before the Lord, saying, 'Behold, the children of Israel have not hearkened unto me; how then shall Pharaoh hear me, who am of uncircumcised lips?' ¹³And the Lord spake unto Moses and unto Aaron, and gave them a charge unto the children of Israel, and unto Pharaoh king of Egypt, to bring the children of Israel out of the land of Egypt. ¹⁴These be the heads of their fathers' houses: the sons of Reuben the firstborn of Israel; Hanoch, and Pallu, Hezron, and Carmi; these be the families of Reuben. ¹⁵And the sons of Simeon: Jemuel, and Jamin, and Ohad, and Jachin, and Zohar, and Shaul the son of a Canaanitish woman; these are the families of Simeon. ¹⁶And these are the names of the sons of Levi according to their generations: Gershon, and Kohath, and Merari; and the years of the life of Levi were an hundred thirty and seven years. ¹⁷The sons of Gershon: Libni, and Shimi, according to their families. ¹⁸And the sons of Kohath: Amram, and Izhar, and Hebron, and Uzziel; and the years of the life of Kohath were an hundred thirty and three years. ¹⁹And the sons of Merari: Mahali and Mushi; these are the families of Levi according to their generations. ²⁰And Amram took him Jochebed his father's sister to wife; and she bare him Aaron and Moses; and the years of the life of Amram were an hundred and thirty and seven

years. ²¹And the sons of Izhar: Korah, and Nepheg, and Zichri. ²²And the sons of Uzziel: Mishael, and Elzaphan, and Zithri. ²³And Aaron took him Elisheba, daughter of Amminadab, sister of Naashon, to wife; and she bare him Nadab, and Abihu, Eleazar, and Ithamar. ²⁴And the sons of Korah: Assir, and Elkanah, and Abiasaph; these are the families of the Korhites. ²⁵And Eleazar Aaron's son took him one of the daughters of Putiel to wife; and she bare him Phinehas. These are the heads of the fathers of the Levites according to their families. ²⁶These are that Aaron and Moses, to whom the Lord said, 'Bring out the children of Israel from the land of Egypt according to their armies.' ²⁷These are they which spake to Pharaoh king of Egypt, to bring out the children of Israel from Egypt; these are that Moses and Aaron.

²⁸And it came to pass on the day when the Lord spake unto Moses in the land of Egypt, ²⁹that the Lord spake unto Moses, saying, 'I am the Lord. Speak thou unto Pharaoh king of Egypt all that I say unto thee.' ³⁰And Moses said before the Lord, 'Behold, I am of uncircumcised lips, and how shall Pharaoh hearken unto me?'

7 And the Lord said unto Moses, 'See, I have made thee a god to Pharaoh, and Aaron thy brother shall be thy prophet. ²Thou shalt speak all that I command thee: and Aaron thy brother shall speak unto Pharaoh, that he send the children of Israel out of his land. ³And I will harden Pharaoh's heart, and multiply my signs and my wonders in the land of Egypt. ⁴But Pharaoh shall not hearken unto you, that I may

lay my hand upon Egypt, and bring forth mine armies, and my people the children of Israel, out of the land of Egypt by great judgments. ⁵And the Egyptians shall know that I am the Lord, when I stretch forth mine hand upon Egypt, and bring out the children of Israel from among them.' ⁶And Moses and Aaron did as the Lord commanded them, so did they. ⁷And Moses was fourscore years old, and Aaron fourscore and three years old, when they spake unto Pharaoh.

⁸And the Lord spake unto Moses and unto Aaron, saying, ⁹'When Pharaoh shall speak unto you, saying, "Shew a miracle for you," then thou shalt say unto Aaron, "Take thy rod, and cast it before Pharaoh, and it shall become a serpent."'

¹⁰And Moses and Aaron went in unto Pharaoh, and they did so as the Lord had commanded; and Aaron cast down his rod before Pharaoh, and before his servants, and it became a serpent. ¹¹Then Pharaoh also called the wise men and the sorcerers; now the magicians of Egypt, they also did in like manner with their enchantments. ¹²For they cast down every man his rod, and they became serpents, but Aaron's rod swallowed up their rods. ¹³And he hardened Pharaoh's heart, that he hearkened not unto them, as the Lord had said.

¹⁴And the Lord said unto Moses, 'Pharaoh's heart is hardened, he refuseth to let the people go. ¹⁵Get thee unto Pharaoh in the morning; lo, he goeth out unto the water; and thou shalt stand by the river's brink against he come; and the rod which was turned to a serpent shalt thou take in thine hand. ¹⁶And thou shalt say unto him, "The Lord God of the Hebrews hath sent me unto thee, saying, 'Let my people

go, that they may serve me in the wilderness,' and, behold, hitherto thou wouldest not hear. ¹⁷ Thus saith the Lord, 'In this thou shalt know that I am the Lord: Behold, I will smite with the rod that is in mine hand upon the waters which are in the river, and they shall be turned to blood. ¹⁸And the fish that is in the river shall die, and the river shall stink; and the Egyptians shall lothe to drink of the water of the river.''''

¹⁹And the Lord spake unto Moses, 'Say unto Aaron, "Take thy rod, and stretch out thine hand upon the waters of Egypt, upon their streams, upon their rivers, and upon their ponds, and upon all their pools of water, that they may become blood; and that there may be blood throughout all the land of Egypt, both in vessels of wood, and in vessels of stone."' ²⁰And Moses and Aaron did so, as the Lord commanded; and he lifted up the rod, and smote the waters that were in the river, in the sight of Pharaoh, and in the sight of his servants; and all the waters that were in the river were turned to blood. ²¹And the fish that was in the river died; and the river stank, and the Egyptians could not drink of the water of the river; and there was blood throughout all the land of Egypt. ²²And the magicians of Egypt did so with their enchantments; and Pharaoh's heart was hardened, neither did he hearken unto them, as the Lord had said. ²³And Pharaoh turned and went into his house, neither did he set his heart to this also. ²⁴And all the Egyptians digged round about the river for water to drink; for they could not drink of the water of the river. ²⁵And seven days were fulfilled, after that the Lord had smitten the river.

8 And the Lord spake unto Moses, 'Go unto Pharaoh, and say unto him, "Thus saith the Lord, 'Let my people go, that they may serve me. ²And if thou refuse to let them go, behold, I will smite all thy borders with frogs. ³And the river shall bring forth frogs abundantly, which shall go up and come into thine house, and into thy bed-chamber, and upon thy bed, and into the house of thy servants, and upon thy people, and into thine ovens, and into thy kneadingtroughs. ⁴And the frogs shall come up both on thee, and upon thy people, and upon all thy servants.'"'

⁵And the Lord spake unto Moses, 'Say unto Aaron, "Stretch forth thine hand with thy rod over the streams, over the rivers, and over the ponds, and cause frogs to come up upon the land of Egypt."' ⁶And Aaron stretched out his hand over the waters of Egypt; and the frogs came up, and covered the land of Egypt. ⁷And the magicians did so with their enchantments, and brought up frogs upon the land of Egypt.

⁸Then Pharaoh called for Moses and Aaron, and said, 'Intreat the Lord, that he may take away the frogs from me, and from my people; and I will let the people go, that they may do sacrifice unto the Lord.' ⁹And Moses said unto Pharaoh, 'Glory over me: when shall I intreat for thee, and for thy servants, and for thy people, to destroy the frogs from thee and thy houses, that they may remain in the river only?' ¹⁰And he said, 'Tomorrow.' And he said, 'Be it according to thy word, that thou mayest know that there is none like unto the Lord our God. ¹¹And the frogs shall depart from thee, and from thy houses, and from thy servants, and from thy

people; they shall remain in the river only.' ¹²And Moses and Aaron went out from Pharaoh, and Moses cried unto the Lord because of the frogs which he had brought against Pharaoh. ¹³And the Lord did according to the word of Moses; and the frogs died out of the houses, out of the villages, and out of the fields. ¹⁴And they gathered them together upon heaps, and the land stank. ¹⁵But when Pharaoh saw that there was respite, he hardened his heart, and hearkened not unto them, as the Lord had said.

¹⁶And the Lord said unto Moses, 'Say unto Aaron, "Stretch out thy rod, and smite the dust of the land, that it may become lice throughout all the land of Egypt."' ¹⁷And they did so; for Aaron stretched out his hand with his rod, and smote the dust of the earth, and it became lice in man, and in beast; all the dust of the land became lice throughout all the land of Egypt. ¹⁸And the magicians did so with their enchantments to bring forth lice, but they could not, so there were lice upon man, and upon beast. ¹⁹Then the magicians said unto Pharaoh, 'This is the finger of God' and Pharaoh's heart was hardened, and he hearkened not unto them, as the Lord had said.

²⁰And the Lord said unto Moses, 'Rise up early in the morning, and stand before Pharaoh; lo, he cometh forth to the water; and say unto him, "Thus saith the Lord, 'Let my people go, that they may serve me. ²¹Else, if thou wilt not let my people go, behold, I will send swarms of flies upon thee, and upon thy servants, and upon thy people, and into thy houses: and the houses of the Egyptians shall be full of swarms of flies, and also the ground whereon they are. ²²And I will sever

in that day the land of Goshen, in which my people dwell, that no swarms of flies shall be there; to the end thou mayest know that I am the Lord in the midst of the earth. ²³And I will put a division between my people and thy people: tomorrow shall this sign be.'"' ²⁴And the Lord did so; and there came a grievous swarm of flies into the house of Pharaoh, and into his servants' houses, and into all the land of Egypt: the land was corrupted by reason of the swarm of flies.

²⁵And Pharaoh called for Moses and for Aaron, and said, 'Go ye, sacrifice to your God in the land.' ²⁶And Moses said, 'It is not meet so to do; for we shall sacrifice the abomination of the Egyptians to the Lord our God. Lo, shall we sacrifice the abomination of the Egyptians before their eyes, and will they not stone us? ²⁷ We will go three days' journey into the wilderness, and sacrifice to the Lord our God, as he shall command us.' ²⁸And Pharaoh said, 'I will let you go, that ye may sacrifice to the Lord your God in the wilderness; only ye shall not go very far away. Intreat for me.' ²⁹And Moses said, 'Behold, I go out from thee, and I will intreat the Lord that the swarms of flies may depart from Pharaoh, from his servants, and from his people, tomorrow: but let not Pharaoh deal deceitfully any more in not letting the people go to sacrifice to the Lord.' ³⁰And Moses went out from Pharaoh, and intreated the Lord. ³¹And the Lord did according to the word of Moses; and he removed the swarms of flies from Pharaoh, from his servants, and from his people; there remained not one. ³²And Pharaoh hardened his heart at this time also, neither would he let the people go.

9 Then the Lord said unto Moses, 'Go in unto Pharaoh, and tell him, "Thus saith the Lord God of the Hebrews, 'Let my people go, that they may serve me.' ²For if thou refuse to let them go, and wilt hold them still, ³behold, the hand of the Lord is upon thy cattle which is in the field, upon the horses, upon the asses, upon the camels, upon the oxen, and upon the sheep; there shall be a very grievous murrain. ⁴And the Lord shall sever between the cattle of Israel and the cattle of Egypt, and there shall nothing die of all that is the children's of Israel."' ⁵And the Lord appointed a set time, saying, 'Tomorrow the Lord shall do this thing in the land.' ⁶And the Lord did that thing on the morrow, and all the cattle of Egypt died, but of the cattle of the children of Israel died not one. ⁷And Pharaoh sent, and, behold, there was not one of the cattle of the Israelites dead. And the heart of Pharaoh was hardened, and he did not let the people go.

⁸And the Lord said unto Moses and unto Aaron, 'Take to you handfuls of ashes of the furnace, and let Moses sprinkle it toward the heaven in the sight of Pharaoh. ⁹And it shall become small dust in all the land of Egypt, and shall be a boil breaking forth with blains upon man, and upon beast, throughout all the land of Egypt.' ¹⁰And they took ashes of the furnace, and stood before Pharaoh; and Moses sprinkled it up toward heaven; and it became a boil breaking forth with blains upon man, and upon beast. ¹¹And the magicians could not stand before Moses because of the boils; for the boil was upon the magicians, and upon all the Egyptians. ¹²And the Lord hardened the heart of Pharaoh, and he hearkened not

unto them, as the Lord had spoken unto Moses.

¹³And the Lord said unto Moses, 'Rise up early in the morning, and stand before Pharaoh, and say unto him, "Thus saith the Lord God of the Hebrews, 'Let my people go, that they may serve me. ¹⁴For I will at this time send all my plagues upon thine heart, and upon thy servants, and upon thy people; that thou mayest know that there is none like me in all the earth. ¹⁵For now I will stretch out my hand, that I may smite thee and thy people with pestilence; and thou shalt be cut off from the earth. ¹⁶And in very deed for this cause have I raised thee up, for to shew in thee my power; and that my name may be declared throughout all the earth. ¹⁷As yet exaltest thou thyself against my people, that thou wilt not let them go? ¹⁸Behold, tomorrow about this time I will cause it to rain a very grievous hail, such as hath not been in Egypt since the foundation thereof even until now. ¹⁹Send therefore now, and gather thy cattle, and all that thou hast in the field; for upon every man and beast which shall be found in the field, and shall not be brought home, the hail shall come down upon them, and they shall die.'"' ²⁰He that feared the word of the Lord among the servants of Pharaoh made his servants and his cattle flee into the houses: ²¹and he that regarded not the word of the Lord left his servants and his cattle in the field.

²²And the Lord said unto Moses, 'Stretch forth thine hand toward heaven, that there may be hail in all the land of Egypt, upon man, and upon beast, and upon every herb of the field, throughout the land of Egypt. ²³And Moses stretched forth

his rod toward heaven: and the Lord sent thunder and hail, and the fire ran along upon the ground; and the Lord rained hail upon the land of Egypt.' ²⁴ So there was hail, and fire mingled with the hail, very grievous, such as there was none like it in all the land of Egypt since it became a nation. ²⁵And the hail smote throughout all the land of Egypt all that was in the field, both man and beast; and the hail smote every herb of the field, and brake every tree of the field. ²⁶ Only in the land of Goshen, where the children of Israel were, was there no hail.

²⁷And Pharaoh sent, and called for Moses and Aaron, and said unto them, 'I have sinned this time. The Lord is righteous, and I and my people are wicked. ²⁸ Intreat the Lord (for it is enough) that there be no more mighty thunderings and hail; and I will let you go, and ye shall stay no longer.' ²⁹And Moses said unto him, 'As soon as I am gone out of the city, I will spread abroad my hands unto the Lord; and the thunder shall cease, neither shall there be any more hail; that thou mayest know how that the earth is the Lord's. ³⁰ But as for thee and thy servants, I know that ye will not yet fear the Lord God.' ³¹And the flax and the barley was smitten: for the barley was in the ear, and the flax was bolled. ³² But the wheat and the rie were not smitten, for they were not grown up. ³³And Moses went out of the city from Pharaoh, and spread abroad his hands unto the Lord: and the thunders and hail ceased, and the rain was not poured upon the earth. ³⁴And when Pharaoh saw that the rain and the hail and the thunders were ceased, he sinned yet more, and hardened his

heart, he and his servants. ³⁵And the heart of Pharaoh was hardened, neither would he let the children of Israel go; as the Lord had spoken by Moses.

10 And the Lord said unto Moses, 'Go in unto Pharaoh, for I have hardened his heart, and the heart of his servants, that I might shew these my signs before him; ²and that thou mayest tell in the ears of thy son, and of thy son's son, what things I have wrought in Egypt, and my signs which I have done among them; that ye may know how that I am the Lord.' ³And Moses and Aaron came in unto Pharaoh, and said unto him, 'Thus saith the Lord God of the Hebrews, "How long wilt thou refuse to humble thyself before me? Let my people go, that they may serve me. ⁴Else, if thou refuse to let my people go, behold, tomorrow will I bring the locusts into thy coast. ⁵And they shall cover the face of the earth, that one cannot be able to see the earth; and they shall eat the residue of that which is escaped, which remaineth unto you from the hail, and shall eat every tree which groweth for you out of the field. ⁶And they shall fill thy houses, and the houses of all thy servants, and the houses of all the Egyptians; which neither thy fathers, nor thy fathers' fathers have seen, since the day that they were upon the earth unto this day."' And he turned himself, and went out from Pharaoh. ⁷And Pharaoh's servants said unto him, 'How long shall this man be a snare unto us? Let the men go, that they may serve the Lord their God. Knowest thou not yet that Egypt is destroyed?' ⁸And Moses and Aaron were brought again unto

Pharaoh, and he said unto them, 'Go, serve the Lord your God, but who are they that shall go?' ⁹And Moses said, 'We will go with our young and with our old, with our sons and with our daughters, with our flocks and with our herds will we go; for we must hold a feast unto the Lord.' ¹⁰And he said unto them, 'Let the Lord be so with you, as I will let you go, and your little ones. Look to it; for evil is before you. ¹¹Not so; go now ye that are men, and serve the Lord; for that ye did desire.' And they were driven out from Pharaoh's presence.

¹²And the Lord said unto Moses, 'Stretch out thine hand over the land of Egypt for the locusts, that they may come up upon the land of Egypt, and eat every herb of the land, even all that the hail hath left.' ¹³And Moses stretched forth his rod over the land of Egypt, and the Lord brought an east wind upon the land all that day, and all that night; and when it was morning, the east wind brought the locusts. ¹⁴And the locusts went up over all the land of Egypt, and rested in all the coasts of Egypt: very grievous were they; before them there were no such locusts as they, neither after them shall be such. ¹⁵For they covered the face of the whole earth, so that the land was darkened; and they did eat every herb of the land, and all the fruit of the trees which the hail had left; and there remained not any green thing in the trees, or in the herbs of the field, through all the land of Egypt.

¹⁶Then Pharaoh called for Moses and Aaron in haste; and he said, 'I have sinned against the Lord your God, and against you. ¹⁷Now therefore forgive, I pray thee, my sin only this once, and intreat the Lord your God, that he may take away

from me this death only.' ¹⁸And he went out from Pharaoh, and intreated the Lord. ¹⁹And the Lord turned a mighty strong west wind, which took away the locusts, and cast them into the Red sea; there remained not one locust in all the coasts of Egypt. ²⁰But the Lord hardened Pharaoh's heart, so that he would not let the children of Israel go.

²¹And the Lord said unto Moses, 'Stretch out thine hand toward heaven, that there may be darkness over the land of Egypt, even darkness which may be felt.' ²²And Moses stretched forth his hand toward heaven; and there was a thick darkness in all the land of Egypt three days. ²³They saw not one another, neither rose any from his place for three days, but all the children of Israel had light in their dwellings.

²⁴And Pharaoh called unto Moses, and said, 'Go ye, serve the Lord; only let your flocks and your herds be stayed: let your little ones also go with you.' ²⁵And Moses said, 'Thou must give us also sacrifices and burnt offerings, that we may sacrifice unto the Lord our God. ²⁶Our cattle also shall go with us; there shall not an hoof be left behind; for thereof must we take to serve the Lord our God; and we know not with what we must serve the Lord, until we come thither.'

²⁷But the Lord hardened Pharaoh's heart, and he would not let them go. ²⁸And Pharaoh said unto him, 'Get thee from me, take heed to thyself, see my face no more; for in that day thou seest my face thou shalt die.' ²⁹And Moses said, 'Thou hast spoken well, I will see thy face again no more.'

11 And the Lord said unto Moses, 'Yet will I bring one plague more upon Pharaoh, and upon Egypt; afterwards he will let you go hence: when he shall let you go, he shall surely thrust you out hence altogether. ²Speak now in the ears of the people, and let every man borrow of his neighbour, and every woman of her neighbour, jewels of silver, and jewels of gold.' ³And the Lord gave the people favour in the sight of the Egyptians. Moreover the man Moses was very great in the land of Egypt, in the sight of Pharaoh's servants, and in the sight of the people. ⁴And Moses said, 'Thus saith the Lord, "About midnight will I go out into the midst of Egypt; ⁵and all the firstborn in the land of Egypt shall die, from the firstborn of Pharaoh that sitteth upon his throne, even unto the firstborn of the maidservant that is behind the mill; and all the firstborn of beasts. ⁶And there shall be a great cry throughout all the land of Egypt, such as there was none like it, nor shall be like it any more. ⁷But against any of the children of Israel shall not a dog move his tongue, against man or beast, that ye may know how that the Lord doth put a difference between the Egyptians and Israel." ⁸And all these thy servants shall come down unto me, and bow down themselves unto me, saying, "Get thee out, and all the people that follow thee," and after that I will go out.' And he went out from Pharaoh in a great anger. ⁹And the Lord said unto Moses, 'Pharaoh shall not hearken unto you; that my wonders may be multiplied in the land of Egypt.' ¹⁰And Moses and Aaron did all these wonders before Pharaoh, and the Lord hardened Pharaoh's heart, so that he

would not let the children of Israel go out of his land.

12

And the Lord spake unto Moses and Aaron in the land of Egypt, saying, ²'This month shall be unto you the beginning of months; it shall be the first month of the year to you.

³'Speak ye unto all the congregation of Israel, saying, "In the tenth day of this month they shall take to them every man a lamb, according to the house of their fathers, a lamb for an house. ⁴And if the household be too little for the lamb, let him and his neighbour next unto his house take it according to the number of the souls; every man according to his eating shall make your count for the lamb. ⁵Your lamb shall be without blemish, a male of the first year; ye shall take it out from the sheep, or from the goats. ⁶And ye shall keep it up until the fourteenth day of the same month; and the whole assembly of the congregation of Israel shall kill it in the evening. ⁷And they shall take of the blood, and strike it on the two side posts and on the upper door post of the houses, wherein they shall eat it. ⁸And they shall eat the flesh in that night, roast with fire, and unleavened bread; and with bitter herbs they shall eat it. ⁹Eat not of it raw, nor sodden at all with water, but roast with fire; his head with his legs, and with the purtenance thereof. ¹⁰And ye shall let nothing of it remain until the morning; and that which remaineth of it until the morning ye shall burn with fire.

¹¹'"And thus shall ye eat it; with your loins girded, your shoes on your feet, and your staff in your hand; and ye shall eat it in haste; it is the Lord's passover. ¹²For I will pass

through the land of Egypt this night, and will smite all the firstborn in the land of Egypt, both man and beast; and against all the gods of Egypt I will execute judgment: I am the Lord. ¹³And the blood shall be to you for a token upon the houses where ye are: and when I see the blood, I will pass over you, and the plague shall not be upon you to destroy you, when I smite the land of Egypt. ¹⁴And this day shall be unto you for a memorial; and ye shall keep it a feast to the Lord throughout your generations; ye shall keep it a feast by an ordinance for ever. ¹⁵Seven days shall ye eat unleavened bread; even the first day ye shall put away leaven out of your houses; for whosoever eateth leavened bread from the first day until the seventh day, that soul shall be cut off from Israel. ¹⁶And in the first day there shall be an holy convocation, and in the seventh day there shall be an holy convocation to you; no manner of work shall be done in them, save that which every man must eat, that only may be done of you. ¹⁷And ye shall observe the feast of unleavened bread; for in this self-same day have I brought your armies out of the land of Egypt; therefore shall ye observe this day in your generations by an ordinance for ever.

¹⁸ '"In the first month, on the fourteenth day of the month at even, ye shall eat unleavened bread, until the one and twentieth day of the month at even. ¹⁹Seven days shall there be no leaven found in your houses: for whosoever eateth that which is leavened, even that soul shall be cut off from the congregation of Israel, whether he be a stranger, or born in the land. ²⁰Ye shall eat nothing leavened; in all

your habitations shall ye eat unleavened bread."'

²¹ Then Moses called for all the elders of Israel, and said unto them, 'Draw out and take you a lamb according to your families, and kill the passover. ²² And ye shall take a bunch of hyssop, and dip it in the blood that is in the bason, and strike the lintel and the two side posts with the blood that is in the bason; and none of you shall go out at the door of his house until the morning. ²³ For the Lord will pass through to smite the Egyptians; and when he seeth the blood upon the lintel, and on the two side posts, the Lord will pass over the door, and will not suffer the destroyer to come in unto your houses to smite you. ²⁴ And ye shall observe this thing for an ordinance to thee and to thy sons for ever. ²⁵ And it shall come to pass, when ye be come to the land which the Lord will give you, according as he hath promised, that ye shall keep this service. ²⁶ And it shall come to pass, when your children shall say unto you, "What mean ye by this service?" ²⁷ That ye shall say, "It is the sacrifice of the Lord's passover, who passed over the houses of the children of Israel in Egypt, when he smote the Egyptians, and delivered our houses."' And the people bowed the head and worshipped. ²⁸ And the children of Israel went away, and did as the Lord had commanded Moses and Aaron, so did they.

²⁹ And it came to pass, that at midnight the Lord smote all the firstborn in the land of Egypt, from the firstborn of Pharaoh that sat on his throne unto the firstborn of the captive that was in the dungeon; and all the firstborn of cattle. ³⁰ And Pharaoh rose up in the night, he, and all his servants, and all

the Egyptians; and there was a great cry in Egypt; for there was not a house where there was not one dead.

³¹And he called for Moses and Aaron by night, and said, 'Rise up, and get you forth from among my people, both ye and the children of Israel; and go, serve the Lord, as ye have said. ³²Also take your flocks and your herds, as ye have said, and be gone; and bless me also.' ³³And the Egyptians were urgent upon the people, that they might send them out of the land in haste; for they said, 'We be all dead men.' ³⁴And the people took their dough before it was leavened, their kneading-troughs being bound up in their clothes upon their shoulders. ³⁵And the children of Israel did according to the word of Moses; and they borrowed of the Egyptians jewels of silver, and jewels of gold, and raiment. ³⁶And the Lord gave the people favour in the sight of the Egyptians, so that they lent unto them such things as they required. And they spoiled the Egyptians.

³⁷And the children of Israel journeyed from Rameses to Succoth, about six hundred thousand on foot that were men, beside children. ³⁸And a mixed multitude went up also with them; and flocks, and herds, even very much cattle. ³⁹And they baked unleavened cakes of the dough which they brought forth out of Egypt, for it was not leavened; because they were thrust out of Egypt, and could not tarry, neither had they prepared for themselves any victual.

⁴⁰Now the sojourning of the children of Israel, who dwelt in Egypt, was four hundred and thirty years. ⁴¹And it came to pass at the end of the four hundred and thirty years, even

the selfsame day it came to pass, that all the hosts of the Lord went out from the land of Egypt. ⁴²It is a night to be much observed unto the Lord for bringing them out from the land of Egypt. This is that night of the Lord to be observed of all the children of Israel in their generations.

⁴³And the Lord said unto Moses and Aaron, 'This is the ordinance of the passover. There shall no stranger eat thereof; ⁴⁴but every man's servant that is bought for money, when thou hast circumcised him, then shall he eat thereof. ⁴⁵A foreigner and an hired servant shall not eat thereof. ⁴⁶In one house shall it be eaten; thou shalt not carry forth ought of the flesh abroad out of the house; neither shall ye break a bone thereof. ⁴⁷All the congregation of Israel shall keep it. ⁴⁸And when a stranger shall sojourn with thee, and will keep the passover to the Lord, let all his males be circumcised, and then let him come near and keep it; and he shall be as one that is born in the land, for no uncircumcised person shall eat thereof. ⁴⁹One law shall be to him that is homeborn, and unto the stranger that sojourneth among you.' ⁵⁰Thus did all the children of Israel; as the Lord commanded Moses and Aaron, so did they. ⁵¹And it came to pass the selfsame day, that the Lord did bring the children of Israel out of the land of Egypt by their armies.

13 And the Lord spake unto Moses, saying, ²'Sanctify unto me all the firstborn, whatsoever openeth the womb among the children of Israel, both of man and of beast: it is mine.'

³And Moses said unto the people, 'Remember this day, in

which ye came out from Egypt, out of the house of bondage; for by strength of hand the Lord brought you out from this place; there shall no leavened bread be eaten. ⁴ This day came ye out in the month Abib.

⁵ 'And it shall be when the Lord shall bring thee into the land of the Canaanites, and the Hittites, and the Amorites, and the Hivites, and the Jebusites, which he sware unto thy fathers to give thee, a land flowing with milk and honey, that thou shalt keep this service in this month. ⁶ Seven days thou shalt eat unleavened bread, and in the seventh day shall be a feast to the Lord. ⁷ Unleavened bread shall be eaten seven days; and there shall no leavened bread be seen with thee, neither shall there be leaven seen with thee in all thy quarters.

⁸ 'And thou shalt shew thy son in that day, saying, "This is done because of that which the Lord did unto me when I came forth out of Egypt." ⁹ And it shall be for a sign unto thee upon thine hand, and for a memorial between thine eyes, that the Lord's law may be in thy mouth; for with a strong hand hath the Lord brought thee out of Egypt. ¹⁰ Thou shalt therefore keep this ordinance in his season from year to year.

¹¹ 'And it shall be when the Lord shall bring thee into the land of the Canaanites, as he sware unto thee and to thy fathers, and shall give it thee, ¹² that thou shalt set apart unto the Lord all that openeth the matrix, and every firstling that cometh of a beast which thou hast; the males shall be the Lord's. ¹³ And every firstling of an ass thou shalt redeem with a lamb; and if thou wilt not redeem it, then thou shalt break his neck; and all the firstborn of man among thy children

shalt thou redeem.

¹⁴'And it shall be when thy son asketh thee in time to come, saying, "What is this?" that thou shalt say unto him, "By strength of hand the Lord brought us out from Egypt, from the house of bondage: ¹⁵And it came to pass, when Pharaoh would hardly let us go, that the Lord slew all the firstborn in the land of Egypt, both the firstborn of man, and the firstborn of beast; therefore I sacrifice to the Lord all that openeth the matrix, being males; but all the firstborn of my children I redeem." ¹⁶And it shall be for a token upon thine hand, and for frontlets between thine eyes, for by strength of hand the Lord brought us forth out of Egypt.'

¹⁷And it came to pass, when Pharaoh had let the people go, that God led them not through the way of the land of the Philistines, although that was near; for God said, 'Lest per-adventure the people repent when they see war, and they return to Egypt.' ¹⁸But God led the people about, through the way of the wilderness of the Red sea, and the children of Israel went up harnessed out of the land of Egypt. ¹⁹And Moses took the bones of Joseph with him, for he had straitly sworn the children of Israel, saying, 'God will surely visit you; and ye shall carry up my bones away hence with you.'

²⁰And they took their journey from Succoth, and encamped in Etham, in the edge of the wilderness. ²¹And the Lord went before them by day in a pillar of a cloud, to lead them the way; and by night in a pillar of fire, to give them light; to go by day and night. ²²He took not away the pillar of the cloud by day, nor the pillar of fire by night, from before the people.

14 And the Lord spake unto Moses, saying, ²"Speak unto the children of Israel, that they turn and encamp before Pi-hahiroth, between Migdol and the sea, over against Baal-zephon; before it shall ye encamp by the sea. ³For Pharaoh will say of the children of Israel, "They are entangled in the land, the wilderness hath shut them in." ⁴And I will harden Pharaoh's heart, that he shall follow after them; and I will be honoured upon Pharaoh, and upon all his host; that the Egyptians may know that I am the Lord.' And they did so.

⁵And it was told the king of Egypt that the people fled; and the heart of Pharaoh and of his servants was turned against the people, and they said, 'Why have we done this, that we have let Israel go from serving us?' ⁶And he made ready his chariot, and took his people with him. ⁷And he took six hundred chosen chariots, and all the chariots of Egypt, and captains over every one of them. ⁸And the Lord hardened the heart of Pharaoh king of Egypt, and he pursued after the children of Israel: and the children of Israel went out with an high hand. ⁹But the Egyptians pursued after them, all the horses and chariots of Pharaoh, and his horsemen, and his army, and overtook them encamping by the sea, beside Pi-hahiroth, before Baal-zephon.

¹⁰And when Pharaoh drew nigh, the children of Israel lifted up their eyes, and, behold, the Egyptians marched after them; and they were sore afraid; and the children of Israel cried out unto the Lord. ¹¹And they said unto Moses, 'Because there were no graves in Egypt, hast thou taken us away to

die in the wilderness? Wherefore hast thou dealt thus with us, to carry us forth out of Egypt? ¹²Is not this the word that we did tell thee in Egypt, saying, "Let us alone, that we may serve the Egyptians"? For it had been better for us to serve the Egyptians, than that we should die in the wilderness.'

¹³And Moses said unto the people, 'Fear ye not, stand still, and see the salvation of the Lord, which he will shew to you today, for the Egyptians whom ye have seen to day, ye shall see them again no more for ever. ¹⁴The Lord shall fight for you, and ye shall hold your peace.'

¹⁵And the Lord said unto Moses, 'Wherefore criest thou unto me? Speak unto the children of Israel, that they go forward; ¹⁶but lift thou up thy rod, and stretch out thine hand over the sea, and divide it, and the children of Israel shall go on dry ground through the midst of the sea. ¹⁷And I, behold, I will harden the hearts of the Egyptians, and they shall follow them; and I will get me honour upon Pharaoh, and upon all his host, upon his chariots, and upon his horsemen. ¹⁸And the Egyptians shall know that I am the Lord, when I have gotten me honour upon Pharaoh, upon his chariots, and upon his horsemen.'

¹⁹And the angel of God, which went before the camp of Israel, removed and went behind them; and the pillar of the cloud went from before their face, and stood behind them. ²⁰And it came between the camp of the Egyptians and the camp of Israel; and it was a cloud and darkness to them, but it gave light by night to these; so that the one came not near the other all the night. ²¹And Moses stretched out his hand

over the sea; and the Lord caused the sea to go back by a strong east wind all that night, and made the sea dry land, and the waters were divided. ²²And the children of Israel went into the midst of the sea upon the dry ground, and the waters were a wall unto them on their right hand, and on their left.

²³And the Egyptians pursued, and went in after them to the midst of the sea, even all Pharaoh's horses, his chariots, and his horsemen. ²⁴And it came to pass, that in the morning watch the Lord looked unto the host of the Egyptians through the pillar of fire and of the cloud, and troubled the host of the Egyptians, ²⁵and took off their chariot wheels, that they drave them heavily, so that the Egyptians said, 'Let us flee from the face of Israel; for the Lord fighteth for them against the Egyptians.'

²⁶And the Lord said unto Moses, 'Stretch out thine hand over the sea, that the waters may come again upon the Egyptians, upon their chariots, and upon their horsemen.' ²⁷And Moses stretched forth his hand over the sea, and the sea returned to his strength when the morning appeared; and the Egyptians fled against it; and the Lord overthrew the Egyptians in the midst of the sea. ²⁸And the waters returned, and covered the chariots, and the horsemen, and all the host of Pharaoh that came into the sea after them; there remained not so much as one of them. ²⁹But the children of Israel walked upon dry land in the midst of the sea; and the waters were a wall unto them on their right hand, and on their left. ³⁰Thus the Lord saved Israel that day out of the hand of the Egyptians; and Israel saw the Egyptians dead upon the sea

shore. [31]And Israel saw that great work which the Lord did upon the Egyptians; and the people feared the Lord, and believed the Lord, and his servant Moses.

15 Then sang Moses and the children of Israel this song unto the Lord, and spake, saying,

'I will sing unto the Lord,
    for he hath triumphed gloriously.
        The horse and his rider
    hath he thrown into the sea.
[2]The Lord is my strength and song,
        and he is become my salvation;
    he is my God,
        and I will prepare him an habitation;
    my father's God, and I will exalt him.
[3]The Lord is a man of war; the Lord is his name.
[4]Pharaoh's chariots and his host
    hath he cast into the sea;
        his chosen captains also are drowned
    in the Red sea.
[5]The depths have covered them;
    they sank into the bottom as a stone.
[6]Thy right hand, O Lord,
    is become glorious in power;
        thy right hand, O Lord,
    hath dashed in pieces the enemy.
[7]And in the greatness of thine excellency thou hast
    overthrown them that rose up against thee;

thou sentest forth thy wrath,
which consumed them as stubble.
⁸And with the blast of thy nostrils
the waters were gathered together,
the floods stood upright as an heap,
and the depths were congealed
in the heart of the sea.
⁹ The enemy said, "I will pursue, I will overtake,
I will divide the spoil;
my lust shall be satisfied upon them;
I will draw my sword,
my hand shall destroy them."
¹⁰ Thou didst blow with thy wind,
the sea covered them;
they sank as lead in the mighty waters.
¹¹ Who is like unto thee, O Lord, among the gods?
Who is like thee, glorious in holiness,
fearful in praises, doing wonders?
¹² Thou stretchedst out thy right hand,
the earth swallowed them.
¹³ Thou in thy mercy hast led forth the people
which thou hast redeemed;
thou hast guided them in thy strength
unto thy holy habitation.
¹⁴ The people shall hear, and be afraid;
sorrow shall take hold
on the inhabitants of Palestina.
¹⁵ Then the dukes of Edom shall be amazed;

the mighty men of Moab,
    trembling shall take hold upon them;
    all the inhabitants of Canaan shall melt away.
¹⁶ Fear and dread shall fall upon them;
    by the greatness of thine arm
        they shall be as still as a stone;
till thy people pass over, O Lord,
    till the people pass over,
    which thou hast purchased.
¹⁷ Thou shalt bring them in, and plant them
    in the mountain of thine inheritance,
        in the place, O Lord, which thou hast made
    for thee to dwell in, in the Sanctuary, O Lord,
        which thy hands have established.
¹⁸ The Lord shall reign for ever and ever.'

¹⁹ For the horse of Pharaoh went in with his chariots and with his horsemen into the sea, and the Lord brought again the waters of the sea upon them; but the children of Israel went on dry land in the midst of the sea.

²⁰ And Miriam the prophetess, the sister of Aaron, took a timbrel in her hand; and all the women went out after her with timbrels and with dances. ²¹ And Miriam answered them, 'Sing ye to the Lord, for he hath triumphed gloriously; the horse and his rider hath he thrown into the sea.' ²² So Moses brought Israel from the Red sea, and they went out into the wilderness of Shur; and they went three days in the wilderness, and found no water.

²³ And when they came to Marah, they could not drink of

the waters of Marah, for they were bitter; therefore the name of it was called Marah. ²⁴And the people murmured against Moses, saying, 'What shall we drink?' ²⁵And he cried unto the Lord; and the Lord shewed him a tree, which when he had cast into the waters, the waters were made sweet. There he made for them a statute and an ordinance, and there he proved them, ²⁶and said, 'If thou wilt diligently hearken to the voice of the Lord thy God, and wilt do that which is right in his sight, and wilt give ear to his commandments, and keep all his statutes, I will put none of these diseases upon thee, which I have brought upon the Egyptians, for I am the Lord that healeth thee.'

²⁷And they came to Elim, where were twelve wells of water, and three-score and ten palm trees, and they encamped there by the waters.

16 And they took their journey from Elim, and all the congregation of the children of Israel came unto the wilderness of Sin, which is between Elim and Sinai, on the fifteenth day of the second month after their departing out of the land of Egypt. ²And the whole congregation of the children of Israel murmured against Moses and Aaron in the wilderness: ³And the children of Israel said unto them, 'Would to God we had died by the hand of the Lord in the land of Egypt, when we sat by the flesh pots, and when we did eat bread to the full; for ye have brought us forth into this wilderness, to kill this whole assembly with hunger.'

⁴Then said the Lord unto Moses, 'Behold, I will rain bread

from heaven for you; and the people shall go out and gather a certain rate every day, that I may prove them, whether they will walk in my law, or no. ⁵And it shall come to pass, that on the sixth day they shall prepare that which they bring in; and it shall be twice as much as they gather daily.' ⁶And Moses and Aaron said unto all the children of Israel, 'At even, then ye shall know that the Lord hath brought you out from the land of Egypt, ⁷and in the morning, then ye shall see the glory of the Lord; for that he heareth your murmurings against the Lord: and what are we, that ye murmur against us?' ⁸And Moses said, 'This shall be, when the Lord shall give you in the evening flesh to eat, and in the morning bread to the full; for that the Lord heareth your murmurings which ye murmur against him; and what are we? Your murmurings are not against us, but against the Lord.'

⁹And Moses spake unto Aaron, 'Say unto all the congregation of the children of Israel, "Come near before the Lord: for he hath heard your murmurings."' ¹⁰And it came to pass, as Aaron spake unto the whole congregation of the children of Israel, that they looked toward the wilderness, and, behold, the glory of the Lord appeared in the cloud.

¹¹And the Lord spake unto Moses, saying, ¹²'I have heard the murmurings of the children of Israel; speak unto them, saying, "At even ye shall eat flesh, and in the morning ye shall be filled with bread; and ye shall know that I am the Lord your God."' ¹³And it came to pass, that at even the quails came up, and covered the camp; and in the morning the dew lay round about the host. ¹⁴And when the dew that lay was

gone up, behold, upon the face of the wilderness there lay a small round thing, as small as the hoar frost on the ground. ¹⁵And when the children of Israel saw it, they said one to another, 'It is manna,' for they wist not what it was. And Moses said unto them, 'This is the bread which the Lord hath given you to eat.

¹⁶ 'This is the thing which the Lord hath commanded: "Gather of it every man according to his eating, an omer for every man, according to the number of your persons; take ye every man for them which are in his tents."' ¹⁷And the children of Israel did so, and gathered, some more, some less. ¹⁸And when they did mete it with an omer, he that gathered much had nothing over, and he that gathered little had no lack; they gathered every man according to his eating. ¹⁹And Moses said, 'Let no man leave of it till the morning.' ²⁰Notwithstanding they hearkened not unto Moses; but some of them left of it until the morning, and it bred worms, and stank; and Moses was wroth with them. ²¹And they gathered it every morning, every man according to his eating; and when the sun waxed hot, it melted.

²²And it came to pass, that on the sixth day they gathered twice as much bread, two omers for one man; and all the rulers of the congregation came and told Moses. ²³And he said unto them, 'This is that which the Lord hath said, "Tomorrow is the rest of the holy sabbath unto the Lord. Bake that which ye will bake to day, and seethe that ye will seethe; and that which remaineth over lay up for you to be kept until the morning."' ²⁴And they laid it up till the morning, as Moses

bade; and it did not stink, neither was there any worm therein. ²⁵And Moses said, 'Eat that to day; for today is a sabbath unto the Lord; today ye shall not find it in the field. ²⁶ Six days ye shall gather it; but on the seventh day, which is the sabbath, in it there shall be none.'

²⁷And it came to pass, that there went out some of the people on the seventh day for to gather, and they found none. ²⁸And the Lord said unto Moses, 'How long refuse ye to keep my commandments and my laws? ²⁹ See, for that the Lord hath given you the sabbath, therefore he giveth you on the sixth day the bread of two days; abide ye every man in his place, let no man go out of his place on the seventh day.' ³⁰ So the people rested on the seventh day. ³¹And the house of Israel called the name thereof Manna; and it was like coriander seed, white; and the taste of it was like wafers made with honey.

³²And Moses said, 'This is the thing which the Lord commandeth: "Fill an omer of it to be kept for your generations; that they may see the bread wherewith I have fed you in the wilderness, when I brought you forth from the land of Egypt."' ³³And Moses said unto Aaron, 'Take a pot, and put an omer full of manna therein, and lay it up before the Lord, to be kept for your generations.' ³⁴As the Lord commanded Moses, so Aaron laid it up before the Testimony, to be kept. ³⁵And the children of Israel did eat manna forty years, until they came to a land inhabited; they did eat manna, until they came unto the borders of the land of Canaan. ³⁶ Now an omer is the tenth part of an ephah.

17 And all the congregation of the children of Israel journeyed from the wilderness of Sin, after their journeys,
according to the commandment of the Lord, and pitched in
Rephidim; and there was no water for the people to drink.
² Wherefore the people did chide with Moses, and said, 'Give
us water that we may drink.' And Moses said unto them,
'Why chide ye with me? Wherefore do ye tempt the Lord?'
³And the people thirsted there for water; and the people
murmured against Moses, and said, 'Wherefore is this that
thou hast brought us up out of Egypt, to kill us and our children and our cattle with thirst?' ⁴And Moses cried unto the
Lord, saying, 'What shall I do unto this people? They be
almost ready to stone me.' ⁵And the Lord said unto Moses,
'Go on before the people, and take with thee of the elders of
Israel; and thy rod, wherewith thou smotest the river, take
in thine hand, and go. ⁶ Behold, I will stand before thee there
upon the rock in Horeb; and thou shalt smite the rock, and
there shall come water out of it, that the people may drink.'
And Moses did so in the sight of the elders of Israel. ⁷And he
called the name of the place Massah, and Meribah, because
of the chiding of the children of Israel, and because they
tempted the Lord, saying, 'Is the Lord among us, or not?'

⁸ Then came Amalek, and fought with Israel in Rephidim.
⁹And Moses said unto Joshua, 'Choose us out men, and go
out, fight with Amalek; tomorrow I will stand on the top of
the hill with the rod of God in mine hand.' ¹⁰ So Joshua did as
Moses had said to him, and fought with Amalek; and Moses,
Aaron, and Hur went up to the top of the hill. ¹¹And it came

to pass, when Moses held up his hand, that Israel prevailed, and when he let down his hand, Amalek prevailed. ¹²But Moses' hands were heavy; and they took a stone, and put it under him, and he sat thereon; and Aaron and Hur stayed up his hands, the one on the one side, and the other on the other side; and his hands were steady until the going down of the sun. ¹³And Joshua discomfited Amalek and his people with the edge of the sword. ¹⁴And the Lord said unto Moses, 'Write this for a memorial in a book, and rehearse it in the ears of Joshua: for I will utterly put out the remembrance of Amalek from under heaven.' ¹⁵And Moses built an altar, and called the name of it Jehovah-nissi: ¹⁶ for he said, 'Because the Lord hath sworn that the Lord will have war with Amalek from generation to generation.'

18 When Jethro, the priest of Midian, Moses' father in law, heard of all that God had done for Moses, and for Israel his people, and that the Lord had brought Israel out of Egypt, ²then Jethro, Moses' father in law, took Zipporah, Moses' wife, after he had sent her back, ³and her two sons, of which the name of the one was Gershom; for he said, 'I have been an alien in a strange land,' ⁴and the name of the other was Eliezer; for 'The God of my father,' said he, 'was mine help, and delivered me from the sword of Pharaoh.' ⁵And Jethro, Moses' father in law, came with his sons and his wife unto Moses into the wilderness, where he encamped at the mount of God. ⁶And he said unto Moses, 'I thy father in law Jethro am come unto thee, and thy wife, and her two sons with her.'

⁷And Moses went out to meet his father in law, and did obeisance, and kissed him; and they asked each other of their welfare; and they came into the tent. ⁸And Moses told his father in law all that the Lord had done unto Pharaoh and to the Egyptians for Israel's sake, and all the travail that had come upon them by the way, and how the Lord delivered them. ⁹And Jethro rejoiced for all the goodness which the Lord had done to Israel, whom he had delivered out of the hand of the Egyptians. ¹⁰And Jethro said, 'Blessed be the Lord, who hath delivered you out of the hand of the Egyptians, and out of the hand of Pharaoh, who hath delivered the people from under the hand of the Egyptians. ¹¹Now I know that the Lord is greater than all gods, for in the thing wherein they dealt proudly he was above them.' ¹²And Jethro, Moses' father in law, took a burnt offering and sacrifices for God; and Aaron came, and all the elders of Israel, to eat bread with Moses' father in law before God.

¹³And it came to pass on the morrow, that Moses sat to judge the people: and the people stood by Moses from the morning unto the evening. ¹⁴And when Moses' father in law saw all that he did to the people, he said, 'What is this thing that thou doest to the people? Why sittest thou thyself alone, and all the people stand by thee from morning unto even?' ¹⁵And Moses said unto his father in law, 'Because the people come unto me to enquire of God. ¹⁶ When they have a matter, they come unto me; and I judge between one and another, and I do make them know the statutes of God, and his laws.'

¹⁷And Moses' father in law said unto him, 'The thing that thou doest is not good. ¹⁸Thou wilt surely wear away, both thou, and this people that is with thee, for this thing is too heavy for thee; thou art not able to perform it thyself alone. ¹⁹Hearken now unto my voice, I will give thee counsel, and God shall be with thee. Be thou for the people to Godward, that thou mayest bring the causes unto God. ²⁰And thou shalt teach them ordinances and laws, and shalt shew them the way wherein they must walk, and the work that they must do. ²¹Moreover thou shalt provide out of all the people able men, such as fear God, men of truth, hating covetousness; and place such over them, to be rulers of thousands, and rulers of hundreds, rulers of fifties, and rulers of tens. ²²And let them judge the people at all seasons; and it shall be, that every great matter they shall bring unto thee, but every small matter they shall judge; so shall it be easier for thyself, and they shall bear the burden with thee. ²³If thou shalt do this thing, and God command thee so, then thou shalt be able to endure, and all this people shall also go to their place in peace.' ²⁴So Moses hearkened to the voice of his father in law, and did all that he had said. ²⁵And Moses chose able men out of all Israel, and made them heads over the people, rulers of thousands, rulers of hundreds, rulers of fifties, and rulers of tens. ²⁶And they judged the people at all seasons; the hard causes they brought unto Moses, but every small matter they judged themselves.

²⁷And Moses let his father in law depart; and he went his way into his own land.

19 In the third month, when the children of Israel were gone forth out of the land of Egypt, the same day came they into the wilderness of Sinai. ²For they were departed from Rephidim, and were come to the desert of Sinai, and had pitched in the wilderness; and there Israel camped before the mount. ³And Moses went up unto God, and the Lord called unto him out of the mountain, saying, 'Thus shalt thou say to the house of Jacob, and tell the children of Israel, ⁴"Ye have seen what I did unto the Egyptians, and how I bare you on eagles' wings, and brought you unto myself. ⁵Now therefore, if ye will obey my voice indeed, and keep my covenant, then ye shall be a peculiar treasure unto me above all people, for all the earth is mine. ⁶And ye shall be unto me a kingdom of priests, and an holy nation." These are the words which thou shalt speak unto the children of Israel.'

⁷And Moses came and called for the elders of the people, and laid before their faces all these words which the Lord commanded him. ⁸And all the people answered together, and said, 'All that the Lord hath spoken we will do.' And Moses returned the words of the people unto the Lord. ⁹And the Lord said unto Moses, 'Lo, I come unto thee in a thick cloud, that the people may hear when I speak with thee, and believe thee for ever.' And Moses told the words of the people unto the Lord.

¹⁰And the Lord said unto Moses, 'Go unto the people, and sanctify them today and tomorrow, and let them wash their clothes, ¹¹and be ready against the third day; for the third day the Lord will come down in the sight of all the people upon

mount Sinai. ¹²And thou shalt set bounds unto the people round about, saying, "Take heed to yourselves, that ye go not up into the mount, or touch the border of it." Whosoever toucheth the mount shall be surely put to death. ¹³ There shall not an hand touch it, but he shall surely be stoned, or shot through; whether it be beast or man, it shall not live. When the trumpet soundeth long, they shall come up to the mount.'

¹⁴And Moses went down from the mount unto the people, and sanctified the people; and they washed their clothes. ¹⁵And he said unto the people, 'Be ready against the third day: come not at your wives.'

¹⁶And it came to pass on the third day in the morning, that there were thunders and lightnings, and a thick cloud upon the mount, and the voice of the trumpet exceeding loud; so that all the people that was in the camp trembled. ¹⁷And Moses brought forth the people out of the camp to meet with God; and they stood at the nether part of the mount. ¹⁸And mount Sinai was altogether on a smoke, because the Lord descended upon it in fire: and the smoke thereof ascended as the smoke of a furnace, and the whole mount quaked greatly. ¹⁹And when the voice of the trumpet sounded long, and waxed louder and louder, Moses spake, and God answered him by a voice. ²⁰And the Lord came down upon mount Sinai, on the top of the mount; and the Lord called Moses up to the top of the mount; and Moses went up. ²¹And the Lord said unto Moses, 'Go down, charge the people, lest they break through unto the Lord to gaze, and many of them perish. ²²And let the priests also, which come near to the

Lord, sanctify themselves, lest the Lord break forth upon them.' ²³And Moses said unto the Lord, 'The people cannot come up to mount Sinai; for thou chargedst us, saying, "Set bounds about the mount, and sanctify it."' ²⁴And the Lord said unto him, 'Away, get thee down, and thou shalt come up, thou, and Aaron with thee, but let not the priests and the people break through to come up unto the Lord, lest he break forth upon them.' ²⁵So Moses went down unto the people, and spake unto them.

20 And God spake all these words, saying, ²'I am the Lord thy God, which have brought thee out of the land of Egypt, out of the house of bondage.

> ³Thou shalt have no other gods before me.
> ⁴Thou shalt not make unto thee any graven image,
>> or any likeness of any thing
>>> that is in heaven above,
>> or that is in the earth beneath,
>>> or that is in the water under the earth.
> ⁵Thou shalt not bow down thyself to them,
>> nor serve them;
>> for I the Lord thy God am a jealous God,
>>> visiting the iniquity of the fathers
>> upon the children unto the third and
>>> fourth generation of them that hate me;
> ⁶and shewing mercy unto thousands of them
>> that love me, and keep my commandments.

⁷ Thou shalt not take the name
  of the Lord thy God in vain;
    for the Lord will not hold him guiltless
  that taketh his name in vain.
⁸ Remember the sabbath day, to keep it holy.
⁹ Six days shalt thou labour, and do all thy work,
¹⁰ But the seventh day is the sabbath
  of the Lord thy God;
    in it thou shalt not do any work, thou,
  nor thy son, nor thy daughter, thy manservant,
    nor thy maidservant, nor thy cattle,
  nor thy stranger that is within thy gates.
¹¹ For in six days the Lord made heaven and earth,
  the sea, and all that in them is,
    and rested the seventh day;
  wherefore the Lord blessed the sabbath day,
    and hallowed it.
¹² Honour thy father and thy mother:
  that thy days may be long upon the land
    which the Lord thy God giveth thee.
¹³ Thou shalt not kill.
¹⁴ Thou shalt not commit adultery.
¹⁵ Thou shalt not steal.
¹⁶ Thou shalt not bear false witness
  against thy neighbour.
¹⁷ Thou shalt not covet thy neighbour's house,
  thou shalt not covet thy neighbour's wife,
    nor his manservant, nor his maidservant,

nor his ox, nor his ass,
nor any thing that is thy neighbour's.'

¹⁸And all the people saw the thunderings, and the lightnings, and the noise of the trumpet, and the mountain smoking; and when the people saw it, they removed, and stood afar off. ¹⁹And they said unto Moses, 'Speak thou with us, and we will hear, but let not God speak with us, lest we die.' ²⁰And Moses said unto the people, 'Fear not, for God is come to prove you, and that his fear may be before your faces, that ye sin not.' ²¹And the people stood afar off, and Moses drew near unto the thick darkness where God was.

²²And the Lord said unto Moses, 'Thus thou shalt say unto the children of Israel, "Ye have seen that I have talked with you from heaven. ²³ Ye shall not make with me gods of silver, neither shall ye make unto you gods of gold.

²⁴ '"An altar of earth thou shalt make unto me, and shalt sacrifice thereon thy burnt offerings, and thy peace offerings, thy sheep, and thine oxen. In all places where I record my name I will come unto thee, and I will bless thee. ²⁵And if thou wilt make me an altar of stone, thou shalt not build it of hewn stone, for if thou lift up thy tool upon it, thou hast polluted it. ²⁶ Neither shalt thou go up by steps unto mine altar, that thy nakedness be not discovered thereon."

21 'Now these are the judgments which thou shalt set before them. ²"If thou buy an Hebrew servant, six years he shall serve, and in the seventh he shall go out free

for nothing. ³If he came in by himself, he shall go out by himself; if he were married, then his wife shall go out with him. ⁴If his master have given him a wife, and she have born him sons or daughters, the wife and her children shall be her master's, and he shall go out by himself. ⁵And if the servant shall plainly say, 'I love my master, my wife, and my children, I will not go out free': ⁶then his master shall bring him unto the judges; he shall also bring him to the door, or unto the door post; and his master shall bore his ear through with an aul; and he shall serve him for ever.

⁷'"And if a man sell his daughter to be a maidservant, she shall not go out as the menservants do. ⁸If she please not her master, who hath betrothed her to himself, then shall he let her be redeemed; to sell her unto a strange nation he shall have no power, seeing he hath dealt deceitfully with her. ⁹And if he have betrothed her unto his son, he shall deal with her after the manner of daughters. ¹⁰If he take him another wife; her food, her raiment, and her duty of marriage, shall he not diminish. ¹¹And if he do not these three unto her, then shall she go out free without money.

¹²'"He that smiteth a man, so that he die, shall be surely put to death. ¹³And if a man lie not in wait, but God deliver him into his hand, then I will appoint thee a place whither he shall flee. ¹⁴But if a man come presumptuously upon his neighbour, to slay him with guile, thou shalt take him from mine altar, that he may die.

¹⁵'"And he that smiteth his father, or his mother, shall be surely put to death.

¹⁶ '"And he that stealeth a man, and selleth him, or if he be found in his hand, he shall surely be put to death.

¹⁷ '"And he that curseth his father, or his mother, shall surely be put to death.

¹⁸ '"And if men strive together, and one smite another with a stone, or with his fist, and he die not, but keepeth his bed, ¹⁹ if he rise again, and walk abroad upon his staff, then shall he that smote him be quit; only he shall pay for the loss of his time, and shall cause him to be thoroughly healed.

²⁰ '"And if a man smite his servant, or his maid, with a rod, and he die under his hand, he shall be surely punished. ²¹ Notwithstanding, if he continue a day or two, he shall not be punished, for he is his money.

²² '"If men strive, and hurt a woman with child, so that her fruit depart from her, and yet no mischief follow, he shall be surely punished, according as the woman's husband will lay upon him; and he shall pay as the judges determine. ²³ And if any mischief follow, then thou shalt give life for life, ²⁴ eye for eye, tooth for tooth, hand for hand, foot for foot, ²⁵ burning for burning, wound for wound, stripe for stripe.

²⁶ '"And if a man smite the eye of his servant, or the eye of his maid, that it perish, he shall let him go free for his eye's sake. ²⁷ And if he smite out his manservant's tooth, or his maidservant's tooth; he shall let him go free for his tooth's sake.

²⁸ '"If an ox gore a man or a woman, that they die, then the ox shall be surely stoned, and his flesh shall not be eaten; but the owner of the ox shall be quit. ²⁹ But if the ox were wont to push with his horn in time past, and it hath been testified to

his owner, and he hath not kept him in, but that he hath killed a man or a woman; the ox shall be stoned, and his owner also shall be put to death. ³⁰ If there be laid on him a sum of money, then he shall give for the ransom of his life whatsoever is laid upon him. ³¹ Whether he have gored a son, or have gored a daughter, according to this judgment shall it be done unto him. ³² If the ox shall push a manservant or a maidservant, he shall give unto their master thirty shekels of silver, and the ox shall be stoned.

³³ '''And if a man shall open a pit, or if a man shall dig a pit, and not cover it, and an ox or an ass fall therein, ³⁴ the owner of the pit shall make it good, and give money unto the owner of them; and the dead beast shall be his.

³⁵ '''And if one man's ox hurt another's, that he die, then they shall sell the live ox, and divide the money of it; and the dead ox also they shall divide. ³⁶ Or if it be known that the ox hath used to push in time past, and his owner hath not kept him in, he shall surely pay ox for ox; and the dead shall be his own.

22 '''If a man shall steal an ox, or a sheep, and kill it, or sell it, he shall restore five oxen for an ox, and four sheep for a sheep.

² '''If a thief be found breaking up, and be smitten that he die, there shall no blood be shed for him. ³ If the sun be risen upon him, there shall be blood shed for him; for he should make full restitution. If he have nothing, then he shall be sold for his theft. ⁴ If the theft be certainly found in his hand alive, whether it be ox, or ass, or sheep, he shall restore double.

⁵'"If a man shall cause a field or vineyard to be eaten, and shall put in his beast, and shall feed in another man's field, of the best of his own field, and of the best of his own vineyard, shall he make restitution.

⁶'"If fire break out, and catch in thorns, so that the stacks of corn, or the standing corn, or the field, be consumed therewith, he that kindled the fire shall surely make restitution.

⁷'"If a man shall deliver unto his neighbour money or stuff to keep, and it be stolen out of the man's house, if the thief be found, let him pay double. ⁸If the thief be not found, then the master of the house shall be brought unto the judges, to see whether he have put his hand unto his neighbour's goods. ⁹For all manner of trespass, whether it be for ox, for ass, for sheep, for raiment, or for any manner of lost thing, which another challengeth to be his, the cause of both parties shall come before the judges; and whom the judges shall condemn, he shall pay double unto his neighbour. ¹⁰If a man deliver unto his neighbour an ass, or an ox, or a sheep, or any beast, to keep, and it die, or be hurt, or driven away, no man seeing it, ¹¹then shall an oath of the Lord be between them both, that he hath not put his hand unto his neighbour's goods, and the owner of it shall accept thereof, and he shall not make it good. ¹²And if it be stolen from him, he shall make restitution unto the owner thereof. ¹³If it be torn in pieces, then let him bring it for witness, and he shall not make good that which was torn.

¹⁴'"And if a man borrow ought of his neighbour, and it be hurt, or die, the owner thereof being not with it, he shall surely

make it good. ¹⁵ But if the owner thereof be with it, he shall not make it good: if it be an hired thing, it came for his hire.

¹⁶ '"And if a man entice a maid that is not betrothed, and lie with her, he shall surely endow her to be his wife. ¹⁷ If her father utterly refuse to give her unto him, he shall pay money according to the dowry of virgins.

¹⁸ '"Thou shalt not suffer a witch to live. ¹⁹ Whosoever lieth with a beast shall surely be put to death.

²⁰ '"He that sacrificeth unto any god, save unto the Lord only, he shall be utterly destroyed.

²¹ '"Thou shalt neither vex a stranger, nor oppress him, for ye were strangers in the land of Egypt.

²² '"Ye shall not afflict any widow, or fatherless child. ²³ If thou afflict them in any wise, and they cry at all unto me, I will surely hear their cry, ²⁴ and my wrath shall wax hot, and I will kill you with the sword; and your wives shall be widows, and your children fatherless.

²⁵ '"If thou lend money to any of my people that is poor by thee, thou shalt not be to him as an usurer, neither shalt thou lay upon him usury. ²⁶ If thou at all take thy neighbour's raiment to pledge, thou shalt deliver it unto him by that the sun goeth down, ²⁷ For that is his covering only, it is his raiment for his skin. Wherein shall he sleep? And it shall come to pass, when he crieth unto me, that I will hear, for I am gracious.

²⁸ '"Thou shalt not revile the gods, nor curse the ruler of thy people.

²⁹ '"Thou shalt not delay to offer the first of thy ripe fruits, and of thy liquors; the firstborn of thy sons shalt thou give

unto me. ³⁰ Likewise shalt thou do with thine oxen, and with thy sheep. Seven days it shall be with his dam; on the eighth day thou shalt give it me.

³¹ '"And ye shall be holy men unto me. Neither shall ye eat any flesh that is torn of beasts in the field; ye shall cast it to the dogs.

23 '"Thou shalt not raise a false report; put not thine hand with the wicked to be an unrighteous witness. ² Thou shalt not follow a multitude to do evil; neither shalt thou speak in a cause to decline after many to wrest judgment. ³ Neither shalt thou countenance a poor man in his cause.

⁴ '"If thou meet thine enemy's ox or his ass going astray, thou shalt surely bring it back to him again. ⁵ If thou see the ass of him that hateth thee lying under his burden, and wouldest forbear to help him, thou shalt surely help with him. ⁶ Thou shalt not wrest the judgment of thy poor in his cause. ⁷ Keep thee far from a false matter; and the innocent and righteous slay thou not, for I will not justify the wicked.

⁸ '"And thou shalt take no gift, for the gift blindeth the wise, and perverteth the words of the righteous.

⁹ '"Also thou shalt not oppress a stranger, for ye know the heart of a stranger, seeing ye were strangers in the land of Egypt. ¹⁰ And six years thou shalt sow thy land, and shalt gather in the fruits thereof, ¹¹ but the seventh year thou shalt let it rest and lie still, that the poor of thy people may eat, and what they leave the beasts of the field shall eat. In like manner thou shalt deal with thy vineyard, and with thy olive-

yard. ¹² Six days thou shalt do thy work, and on the seventh day thou shalt rest, that thine ox and thine ass may rest, and the son of thy handmaid, and the stranger, may be refreshed. ¹³ And in all things that I have said unto you be circumspect, and make no mention of the name of other gods, neither let it be heard out of thy mouth.

¹⁴ '"Three times thou shalt keep a feast unto me in the year. ¹⁵ Thou shalt keep the feast of unleavened bread (thou shalt eat unleavened bread seven days, as I commanded thee, in the time appointed of the month Abib, for in it thou camest out from Egypt, and none shall appear before me empty); ¹⁶ and the feast of harvest, the firstfruits of thy labours, which thou hast sown in the field; and the feast of ingathering, which is in the end of the year, when thou hast gathered in thy labours out of the field. ¹⁷ Three times in the year all thy males shall appear before the Lord God. ¹⁸ Thou shalt not offer the blood of my sacrifice with leavened bread; neither shall the fat of my sacrifice remain until the morning. ¹⁹ The first of the first-fruits of thy land thou shalt bring into the house of the Lord thy God. Thou shalt not seethe a kid in his mother's milk.

²⁰ '"Behold, I send an Angel before thee, to keep thee in the way, and to bring thee into the place which I have pre-pared. ²¹ Beware of him, and obey his voice; provoke him not, for he will not pardon your transgressions, for my name is in him. ²² But if thou shalt indeed obey his voice, and do all that I speak, then I will be an enemy unto thine enemies, and an adversary unto thine adversaries. ²³ For mine Angel shall go before thee, and bring thee in unto the Amorites, and the

Hittites, and the Perizzites, and the Canaanites, the Hivites, and the Jebusites; and I will cut them off. ²⁴Thou shalt not bow down to their gods, nor serve them, nor do after their works; but thou shalt utterly overthrow them, and quite break down their images. ²⁵And ye shall serve the Lord your God, and he shall bless thy bread, and thy water; and I will take sickness away from the midst of thee.

²⁶ '"There shall nothing cast their young, nor be barren, in thy land; the number of thy days I will fulfil. ²⁷I will send my fear before thee, and will destroy all the people to whom thou shalt come, and I will make all thine enemies turn their backs unto thee. ²⁸And I will send hornets before thee, which shall drive out the Hivite, the Canaanite, and the Hittite, from before thee. ²⁹I will not drive them out from before thee in one year, lest the land become desolate, and the beast of the field multiply against thee. ³⁰By little and little I will drive them out from before thee, until thou be increased, and inherit the land. ³¹And I will set thy bounds from the Red sea even unto the sea of the Philistines, and from the desert unto the river, for I will deliver the inhabitants of the land into your hand; and thou shalt drive them out before thee. ³²Thou shalt make no covenant with them, nor with their gods. ³³They shall not dwell in thy land, lest they make thee sin against me, for if thou serve their gods, it will surely be a snare unto thee."'

24 And he said unto Moses, 'Come up unto the Lord, thou, and Aaron, Nadab, and Abihu, and seventy of

the elders of Israel; and worship ye afar off. ²And Moses alone shall come near the Lord, but they shall not come nigh; neither shall the people go up with him.'

³And Moses came and told the people all the words of the Lord, and all the judgments; and all the people answered with one voice, and said, 'All the words which the Lord hath said will we do.' ⁴And Moses wrote all the words of the Lord, and rose up early in the morning, and builded an altar under the hill, and twelve pillars, according to the twelve tribes of Israel. ⁵And he sent young men of the children of Israel, which offered burnt offerings, and sacrificed peace offerings of oxen unto the Lord. ⁶And Moses took half of the blood, and put it in basons; and half of the blood he sprinkled on the altar. ⁷And he took the book of the covenant, and read in the audience of the people; and they said, 'All that the Lord hath said will we do, and be obedient.' ⁸And Moses took the blood, and sprinkled it on the people, and said, 'Behold the blood of the covenant, which the Lord hath made with you concerning all these words.'

⁹Then went up Moses, and Aaron, Nadab, and Abihu, and seventy of the elders of Israel. ¹⁰And they saw the God of Israel. And there was under his feet as it were a paved work of a sapphire stone, and as it were the body of heaven in his clearness. ¹¹And upon the nobles of the children of Israel he laid not his hand; also they saw God, and did eat and drink.

¹²And the Lord said unto Moses, 'Come up to me into the mount, and be there, and I will give thee tables of stone, and a law, and commandments which I have written, that thou

mayest teach them.' ¹³And Moses rose up, and his minister Joshua, and Moses went up into the mount of God. ¹⁴And he said unto the elders, 'Tarry ye here for us, until we come again unto you, and, behold, Aaron and Hur are with you. If any man have any matters to do, let him come unto them.' ¹⁵And Moses went up into the mount, and a cloud covered the mount. ¹⁶And the glory of the Lord abode upon mount Sinai, and the cloud covered it six days; and the seventh day he called unto Moses out of the midst of the cloud. ¹⁷And the sight of the glory of the Lord was like devouring fire on the top of the mount in the eyes of the children of Israel. ¹⁸And Moses went into the midst of the cloud, and gat him up into the mount; and Moses was in the mount forty days and forty nights.

25 And the Lord spake unto Moses, saying, ²'Speak unto the children of Israel, that they bring me an offering; of every man that giveth it willingly with his heart ye shall take my offering. ³And this is the offering which ye shall take of them: gold, and silver, and brass, ⁴and blue, and purple, and scarlet, and fine linen, and goats' hair, ⁵and rams' skins dyed red, and badgers' skins, and shittim wood, ⁶oil for the light, spices for anointing oil, and for sweet incense, ⁷onyx stones, and stones to be set in the ephod, and in the breastplate. ⁸And let them make me a sanctuary, that I may dwell among them. ⁹According to all that I shew thee, after the pattern of the tabernacle, and the pattern of all the instruments thereof, even so shall ye make it.

¹⁰'And they shall make an ark of shittim wood: two cubits

and a half shall be the length thereof, and a cubit and a half the breadth thereof, and a cubit and a half the height thereof. ¹¹And thou shalt overlay it with pure gold, within and without shalt thou overlay it, and shalt make upon it a crown of gold round about. ¹²And thou shalt cast four rings of gold for it, and put them in the four corners thereof; and two rings shall be in the one side of it, and two rings in the other side of it. ¹³And thou shalt make staves of shittim wood, and overlay them with gold. ¹⁴And thou shalt put the staves into the rings by the sides of the ark, that the ark may be borne with them. ¹⁵The staves shall be in the rings of the ark; they shall not be taken from it. ¹⁶And thou shalt put into the ark the testimony which I shall give thee. ¹⁷And thou shalt make a mercy seat of pure gold; two cubits and a half shall be the length thereof, and a cubit and a half the breadth thereof. ¹⁸And thou shalt make two cherubims of gold, of beaten work shalt thou make them, in the two ends of the mercy seat. ¹⁹And make one cherub on the one end, and the other cherub on the other end; even of the mercy seat shall ye make the cherubims on the two ends thereof. ²⁰And the cherubims shall stretch forth their wings on high, covering the mercy seat with their wings, and their faces shall look one to another; toward the mercy seat shall the faces of the cherubims be. ²¹And thou shalt put the mercy seat above upon the ark; and in the ark thou shalt put the testimony that I shall give thee. ²²And there I will meet with thee, and I will commune with thee from above the mercy seat, from between the two cherubims which are upon the ark of the testimony, of all things which I will give thee in commandment unto the children of Israel.

²³ 'Thou shalt also make a table of shittim wood; two cubits shall be the length thereof, and a cubit the breadth thereof, and a cubit and a half the height thereof. ²⁴And thou shalt overlay it with pure gold, and make thereto a crown of gold round about. ²⁵And thou shalt make unto it a border of an hand breadth round about, and thou shalt make a golden crown to the border thereof round about. ²⁶And thou shalt make for it four rings of gold, and put the rings in the four corners that are on the four feet thereof. ²⁷Over against the border shall the rings be for places of the staves to bear the table. ²⁸And thou shalt make the staves of shittim wood, and overlay them with gold, that the table may be borne with them. ²⁹And thou shalt make the dishes thereof, and spoons thereof, and covers thereof, and bowls thereof, to cover withal; of pure gold shalt thou make them. ³⁰And thou shalt set upon the table shewbread before me alway.

³¹'And thou shalt make a candlestick of pure gold; of beaten work shall the candlestick be made. His shaft, and his branches, his bowls, his knops, and his flowers, shall be of the same. ³²And six branches shall come out of the sides of it; three branches of the candlestick out of the one side, and three branches of the candlestick out of the other side; ³³ three bowls made like unto almonds, with a knop and a flower in one branch; and three bowls made like almonds in the other branch, with a knop and a flower; so in the six branches that come out of the candlestick. ³⁴And in the candlestick shall be four bowls made like unto almonds, with their knops and

their flowers. ³⁵And there shall be a knop under two branches of the same, and a knop under two branches of the same, and a knop under two branches of the same, according to the six branches that proceed out of the candlestick. ³⁶Their knops and their branches shall be of the same; all it shall be one beaten work of pure gold. ³⁷And thou shalt make the seven lamps thereof, and they shall light the lamps thereof, that they may give light over against it. ³⁸And the tongs thereof, and the snuffdishes thereof, shall be of pure gold. ³⁹Of a talent of pure gold shall he make it, with all these vessels. ⁴⁰And look that thou make them after their pattern, which was shewed thee in the mount.

26 'Moreover thou shalt make the tabernacle with ten curtains of fine twined linen, and blue, and purple, and scarlet; with cherubims of cunning work shalt thou make them. ²The length of one curtain shall be eight and twenty cubits, and the breadth of one curtain four cubits, and every one of the curtains shall have one measure. ³The five curtains shall be coupled together one to another; and other five curtains shall be coupled one to another. ⁴And thou shalt make loops of blue upon the edge of the one curtain from the selvedge in the coupling; and likewise shalt thou make in the uttermost edge of another curtain, in the coupling of the second. ⁵Fifty loops shalt thou make in the one curtain, and fifty loops shalt thou make in the edge of the curtain that is in the coupling of the second; that the loops may take hold one of another. ⁶And thou shalt make fifty taches of

gold, and couple the curtains together with the taches, and it shall be one tabernacle.

⁷ 'And thou shalt make curtains of goats' hair to be a covering upon the tabernacle; eleven curtains shalt thou make. ⁸ The length of one curtain shall be thirty cubits, and the breadth of one curtain four cubits; and the eleven curtains shall be all of one measure. ⁹ And thou shalt couple five curtains by themselves, and six curtains by themselves, and shalt double the sixth curtain in the forefront of the tabernacle. ¹⁰ And thou shalt make fifty loops on the edge of the one curtain that is outmost in the coupling, and fifty loops in the edge of the curtain which coupleth the second. ¹¹ And thou shalt make fifty taches of brass, and put the taches into the loops, and couple the tent together, that it may be one. ¹² And the remnant that remaineth of the curtains of the tent, the half curtain that remaineth, shall hang over the backside of the tabernacle. ¹³ And a cubit on the one side, and a cubit on the other side of that which remaineth in the length of the curtains of the tent, it shall hang over the sides of the tabernacle on this side and on that side, to cover it. ¹⁴ And thou shalt make a covering for the tent of rams' skins dyed red, and a covering above of badgers' skins.

¹⁵ 'And thou shalt make boards for the tabernacle of shittim wood standing up. ¹⁶ Ten cubits shall be the length of a board, and a cubit and a half shall be the breadth of one board. ¹⁷ Two tenons shall there be in one board, set in order one against another: thus shalt thou make for all the boards of the tabernacle. ¹⁸ And thou shalt make the boards for the

tabernacle, twenty boards on the south side southward. ¹⁹And thou shalt make forty sockets of silver under the twenty boards; two sockets under one board for his two tenons, and two sockets under another board for his two tenons. ²⁰And for the second side of the tabernacle on the north side there shall be twenty boards; ²¹and their forty sockets of silver; two sockets under one board, and two sockets under another board. ²²And for the sides of the tabernacle westward thou shalt make six boards. ²³And two boards shalt thou make for the corners of the tabernacle in the two sides. ²⁴And they shall be coupled together beneath, and they shall be coupled together above the head of it unto one ring; thus shall it be for them both; they shall be for the two corners. ²⁵And they shall be eight boards, and their sockets of silver, sixteen sockets; two sockets under one board, and two sockets under another board.

²⁶'And thou shalt make bars of shittim wood; five for the boards of the one side of the tabernacle, ²⁷and five bars for the boards of the other side of the tabernacle, and five bars for the boards of the side of the tabernacle, for the two sides westward. ²⁸And the middle bar in the midst of the boards shall reach from end to end. ²⁹And thou shalt overlay the boards with gold, and make their rings of gold for places for the bars, and thou shalt overlay the bars with gold. ³⁰And thou shalt rear up the tabernacle according to the fashion thereof which was shewed thee in the mount.

³¹'And thou shalt make a vail of blue, and purple, and scarlet, and fine twined linen of cunning work; with cherubims

shall it be made; ³² and thou shalt hang it upon four pillars of shittim wood overlaid with gold. Their hooks shall be of gold, upon the four sockets of silver.

³³ 'And thou shalt hang up the vail under the taches, that thou mayest bring in thither within the vail the ark of the testimony; and the vail shall divide unto you between the holy place and the most holy. ³⁴ And thou shalt put the mercy seat upon the ark of the testimony in the most holy place. ³⁵ And thou shalt set the table without the vail, and the candlestick over against the table on the side of the tabernacle toward the south; and thou shalt put the table on the north side. ³⁶ And thou shalt make an hanging for the door of the tent, of blue, and purple, and scarlet, and fine twined linen, wrought with needlework. ³⁷ And thou shalt make for the hanging five pillars of shittim wood, and overlay them with gold, and their hooks shall be of gold, and thou shalt cast five sockets of brass for them.

27

'And thou shalt make an altar of shittim wood, five cubits long, and five cubits broad; the altar shall be foursquare, and the height thereof shall be three cubits. ² And thou shalt make the horns of it upon the four corners thereof; his horns shall be of the same; and thou shalt overlay it with brass. ³ And thou shalt make his pans to receive his ashes, and his shovels, and his basons, and his fleshhooks, and his firepans; all the vessels thereof thou shalt make of brass. ⁴ And thou shalt make for it a grate of network of brass; and upon the net shalt thou make four brasen rings in the four corners thereof. ⁵And thou shalt put it under the compass of the altar beneath, that the net may be even to the midst of the altar. ⁶And thou shalt make staves for the altar, staves of shittim wood, and overlay them with brass. ⁷And the staves shall be put into the rings, and the staves shall be upon the two sides of the altar, to bear it. ⁸Hollow with boards shalt thou make it; as it was shewed thee in the mount, so shall they make it.

⁹'And thou shalt make the court of the tabernacle; for the south side southward there shall be hangings for the court of fine twined linen of an hundred cubits long for one side. ¹⁰And the twenty pillars thereof and their twenty sockets shall be of brass; the hooks of the pillars and their fillets shall be of silver. ¹¹And likewise for the north side in length there shall be hangings of an hundred cubits long, and his twenty pillars and their twenty sockets of brass; the hooks of the pillars and their fillets of silver.

¹²'And for the breadth of the court on the west side shall be hangings of fifty cubits; their pillars ten, and their sockets ten. ¹³And the breadth of the court on the east side eastward shall be fifty cubits. ¹⁴The hangings of one side of the gate shall be fifteen cubits; their pillars three, and their sockets three. ¹⁵And on the other side shall be hangings fifteen cubits: their pillars three, and their sockets three.

¹⁶'And for the gate of the court shall be an hanging of twenty cubits, of blue, and purple, and scarlet, and fine twined linen, wrought with needlework; and their pillars shall be four, and their sockets four. ¹⁷All the pillars round about the

court shall be filleted with silver; their hooks shall be of silver, and their sockets of brass.

¹⁸ 'The length of the court shall be an hundred cubits, and the breadth fifty every where, and the height five cubits of fine twined linen, and their sockets of brass. ¹⁹All the vessels of the tabernacle in all the service thereof, and all the pins thereof, and all the pins of the court, shall be of brass.

²⁰ 'And thou shalt command the children of Israel, that they bring thee pure oil olive beaten for the light, to cause the lamp to burn always. ²¹ In the tabernacle of the congregation without the vail, which is before the testimony, Aaron and his sons shall order it from evening to morning before the Lord; it shall be a statute for ever unto their generations on the behalf of the children of Israel.

28

'And take thou unto thee Aaron thy brother, and his sons with him, from among the children of Israel, that he may minister unto me in the priest's office, even Aaron, Nadab and Abihu, Eleazar and Ithamar, Aaron's sons. ²And thou shalt make holy garments for Aaron thy brother for glory and for beauty. ³And thou shalt speak unto all that are wise hearted, whom I have filled with the spirit of wisdom, that they may make Aaron's garments to consecrate him, that he may minister unto me in the priest's office. ⁴And these are the garments which they shall make: a breastplate, and an ephod, and a robe, and a broidered coat, a mitre, and a girdle; and they shall make holy garments for Aaron thy brother, and his sons, that he may minister unto me in the priest's office. ⁵And they shall take gold, and blue, and purple, and scarlet, and fine linen.

⁶'And they shall make the ephod of gold, of blue, and of purple, of scarlet, and fine twined linen, with cunning work. ⁷It shall have the two shoulderpieces thereof joined at the two edges thereof; and so it shall be joined together. ⁸And the curious girdle of the ephod, which is upon it, shall be of the same, according to the work thereof; even of gold, of blue, and purple, and scarlet, and fine twined linen. ⁹And thou shalt take two onyx stones, and grave on them the names of the children of Israel; ¹⁰six of their names on one stone, and the other six names of the rest on the other stone, according to their birth. ¹¹With the work of an engraver in stone, like the engravings of a signet, shalt thou engrave the two stones with the names of the children of Israel; thou shalt make them to be set in ouches of gold. ¹²And thou shalt put the two stones upon the shoulders of the ephod for stones of memorial unto the children of Israel: and Aaron shall bear their names before the Lord upon his two shoulders for a memorial.

¹³'And thou shalt make ouches of gold, ¹⁴and two chains of pure gold at the ends; of wreathen work shalt thou make them, and fasten the wreathen chains to the ouches.

¹⁵'And thou shalt make the breastplate of judgment with cunning work; after the work of the ephod thou shalt make it; of gold, of blue, and of purple, and of scarlet, and of fine twined linen, shalt thou make it. ¹⁶Foursquare it shall be being doubled; a span shall be the length thereof, and a span

shall be the breadth thereof. ¹⁷And thou shalt set in it settings of stones, even four rows of stones. The first row shall be a sardius, a topaz, and a carbuncle; this shall be the first row. ¹⁸And the second row shall be an emerald, a sapphire, and a diamond. ¹⁹And the third row a ligure, an agate, and an amethyst. ²⁰And the fourth row a beryl, and an onyx, and a jasper; they shall be set in gold in their inclosings. ²¹And the stones shall be with the names of the children of Israel, twelve, according to their names, like the engravings of a signet; every one with his name shall they be according to the twelve tribes.

²²'And thou shalt make upon the breastplate chains at the ends of wreathen work of pure gold. ²³And thou shalt make upon the breastplate two rings of gold, and shalt put the two rings on the two ends of the breastplate. ²⁴And thou shalt put the two wreathen chains of gold in the two rings which are on the ends of the breastplate. ²⁵And the other two ends of the two wreathen chains thou shalt fasten in the two ouches, and put them on the shoulderpieces of the ephod before it.

²⁶'And thou shalt make two rings of gold, and thou shalt put them upon the two ends of the breastplate in the border thereof, which is in the side of the ephod inward. ²⁷And two other rings of gold thou shalt make, and shalt put them on the two sides of the ephod underneath, toward the forepart thereof, over against the other coupling thereof, above the curious girdle of the ephod. ²⁸And they shall bind the breastplate by the rings thereof unto the rings of the ephod with a lace of blue, that it may be above the curious girdle of the

ephod, and that the breastplate be not loosed from the ephod. ²⁹And Aaron shall bear the names of the children of Israel in the breastplate of judgment upon his heart, when he goeth in unto the holy place, for a memorial before the Lord continually.

³⁰ 'And thou shalt put in the breast-plate of judgment the Urim and the Thummim; and they shall be upon Aaron's heart, when he goeth in before the Lord; and Aaron shall bear the judgment of the children of Israel upon his heart before the Lord continually.

³¹ 'And thou shalt make the robe of the ephod all of blue. ³²And there shall be an hole in the top of it, in the midst thereof; it shall have a binding of woven work round about the hole of it, as it were the hole of an habergeon, that it be not rent.

³³ 'And beneath upon the hem of it thou shalt make pomegranates of blue, and of purple, and of scarlet, round about the hem thereof; and bells of gold between them round about: ³⁴ a golden bell and a pomegranate, a golden bell and a pomegranate, upon the hem of the robe round about. ³⁵And it shall be upon Aaron to minister; and his sound shall be heard when he goeth in unto the holy place before the Lord, and when he cometh out, that he die not.

³⁶ 'And thou shalt make a plate of pure gold, and grave upon it, like the engravings of a signet, "Holiness to the Lord" ³⁷and thou shalt put it on a blue lace, that it may be upon the mitre; upon the forefront of the mitre it shall be. ³⁸And it shall be upon Aaron's forehead, that Aaron may bear the iniquity of the holy things, which the children of Israel shall hallow in all their holy gifts; and it shall be always upon his

forehead, that they may be accepted before the Lord.

³⁹ 'And thou shalt embroider the coat of fine linen, and thou shalt make the mitre of fine linen, and thou shalt make the girdle of needlework.

⁴⁰ 'And for Aaron's sons thou shalt make coats, and thou shalt make for them girdles, and bonnets shalt thou make for them, for glory and for beauty. ⁴¹And thou shalt put them upon Aaron thy brother, and his sons with him; and shalt anoint them, and consecrate them, and sanctify them, that they may minister unto me in the priest's office. ⁴²And thou shalt make them linen breeches to cover their nakedness; from the loins even unto the thighs they shall reach. ⁴³And they shall be upon Aaron, and upon his sons, when they come in unto the tabernacle of the congregation, or when they come near unto the altar to minister in the holy place; that they bear not iniquity, and die; it shall be a statute for ever unto him and his seed after him.

29 'And this is the thing that thou shalt do unto them to hallow them, to minister unto me in the priest's office: take one young bullock, and two rams without blemish, ²and unleavened bread, and cakes unleavened tempered with oil, and wafers unleavened anointed with oil; of wheaten flour shalt thou make them. ³And thou shalt put them into one basket, and bring them in the basket, with the bullock and the two rams. ⁴And Aaron and his sons thou shalt bring unto the door of the tabernacle of the congregation, and shalt wash them with water. ⁵And thou shalt take

the garments, and put upon Aaron the coat, and the robe of the ephod, and the ephod, and the breastplate, and gird him with the curious girdle of the ephod. ⁶And thou shalt put the mitre upon his head, and put the holy crown upon the mitre. ⁷Then shalt thou take the anointing oil, and pour it upon his head, and anoint him. ⁸And thou shalt bring his sons, and put coats upon them. ⁹And thou shalt gird them with girdles, Aaron and his sons, and put the bonnets on them; and the priest's office shall be theirs for a perpetual statute; and thou shalt consecrate Aaron and his sons. ¹⁰And thou shalt cause a bullock to be brought before the tabernacle of the congregation; and Aaron and his sons shall put their hands upon the head of the bullock. ¹¹And thou shalt kill the bullock before the Lord, by the door of the tabernacle of the congregation. ¹²And thou shalt take of the blood of the bullock, and put it upon the horns of the altar with thy finger, and pour all the blood beside the bottom of the altar. ¹³And thou shalt take all the fat that covereth the inwards, and the caul that is above the liver, and the two kidneys, and the fat that is upon them, and burn them upon the altar. ¹⁴But the flesh of the bullock, and his skin, and his dung, shalt thou burn with fire without the camp; it is a sin offering.

¹⁵'Thou shalt also take one ram; and Aaron and his sons shall put their hands upon the head of the ram. ¹⁶And thou shalt slay the ram, and thou shalt take his blood, and sprinkle it round about upon the altar. ¹⁷And thou shalt cut the ram in pieces, and wash the inwards of him, and his legs, and put them unto his pieces, and unto his head. ¹⁸And thou

shalt burn the whole ram upon the altar; it is a burnt offering unto the Lord; it is a sweet savour, an offering made by fire unto the Lord.

¹⁹ 'And thou shalt take the other ram; and Aaron and his sons shall put their hands upon the head of the ram. ²⁰ Then shalt thou kill the ram, and take of his blood, and put it upon the tip of the right ear of Aaron, and upon the tip of the right ear of his sons, and upon the thumb of their right hand, and upon the great toe of their right foot, and sprinkle the blood upon the altar round about. ²¹And thou shalt take of the blood that is upon the altar, and of the anointing oil, and sprinkle it upon Aaron, and upon his garments, and upon his sons, and upon the garments of his sons with him; and he shall be hallowed, and his garments, and his sons, and his sons' garments with him. ²²Also thou shalt take of the ram the fat and the rump, and the fat that covereth the inwards, and the caul above the liver, and the two kidneys, and the fat that is upon them, and the right shoulder; for it is a ram of consecration. ²³And one loaf of bread, and one cake of oiled bread, and one wafer out of the basket of the unleavened bread that is before the Lord. ²⁴And thou shalt put all in the hands of Aaron, and in the hands of his sons; and shalt wave them for a wave offering before the Lord. ²⁵And thou shalt receive them of their hands, and burn them upon the altar for a burnt offering, for a sweet savour before the Lord; it is an offering made by fire unto the Lord. ²⁶And thou shalt take the breast of the ram of Aaron's consecration, and wave it for a wave offering before the Lord, and it shall be thy part.

²⁷And thou shalt sanctify the breast of the wave offering, and the shoulder of the heave offering, which is waved, and which is heaved up, of the ram of the consecration, even of that which is for Aaron, and of that which is for his sons. ²⁸And it shall be Aaron's and his sons' by a statute for ever from the children of Israel, for it is an heave offering: and it shall be an heave offering from the children of Israel of the sacrifice of their peace offerings, even their heave offering unto the Lord.

²⁹'And the holy garments of Aaron shall be his sons' after him, to be anointed therein, and to be consecrated in them. ³⁰And that son that is priest in his stead shall put them on seven days, when he cometh into the tabernacle of the congregation to minister in the holy place.

³¹'And thou shalt take the ram of the consecration, and seethe his flesh in the holy place. ³²And Aaron and his sons shall eat the flesh of the ram, and the bread that is in the basket, by the door of the tabernacle of the congregation. ³³And they shall eat those things wherewith the atonement was made, to consecrate and to sanctify them; but a stranger shall not eat thereof, because they are holy. ³⁴And if ought of the flesh of the consecrations, or of the bread, remain unto the morning, then thou shalt burn the remainder with fire; it shall not be eaten, because it is holy. ³⁵And thus shalt thou do unto Aaron, and to his sons, according to all things which I have commanded thee; seven days shalt thou consecrate them. ³⁶And thou shalt offer every day a bullock for a sin offering for atonement; and thou shalt cleanse the altar, when

thou hast made an atonement for it, and thou shalt anoint it, to sanctify it. ³⁷ Seven days thou shalt make an atonement for the altar, and sanctify it; and it shall be an altar most holy; whatsoever toucheth the altar shall be holy.

³⁸ 'Now this is that which thou shalt offer upon the altar: two lambs of the first year day by day continually. ³⁹ The one lamb thou shalt offer in the morning; and the other lamb thou shalt offer at even. ⁴⁰ And with the one lamb a tenth deal of flour mingled with the fourth part of an hin of beaten oil; and the fourth part of an hin of wine for a drink offering. ⁴¹ And the other lamb thou shalt offer at even, and shalt do thereto according to the meat offering of the morning, and according to the drink offering thereof, for a sweet savour, an offering made by fire unto the Lord. ⁴² This shall be a continual burnt offering throughout your generations at the door of the tabernacle of the congregation before the Lord, where I will meet you, to speak there unto thee. ⁴³ And there I will meet with the children of Israel, and the tabernacle shall be sanctified by my glory. ⁴⁴ And I will sanctify the tabernacle of the congregation, and the altar. I will sanctify also both Aaron and his sons, to minister to me in the priest's office.

⁴⁵ 'And I will dwell among the children of Israel, and will be their God. ⁴⁶ And they shall know that I am the Lord their God, that brought them forth out of the land of Egypt, that I may dwell among them. I am the Lord their God.

30 'And thou shalt make an altar to burn incense upon; of shittim wood shalt thou make it. ² A cubit shall be

the length thereof, and a cubit the breadth thereof; four-square shall it be. And two cubits shall be the height thereof; the horns thereof shall be of the same. ³And thou shalt overlay it with pure gold, the top thereof, and the sides thereof round about, and the horns thereof; and thou shalt make unto it a crown of gold round about. ⁴And two golden rings shalt thou make to it under the crown of it, by the two corners thereof, upon the two sides of it shalt thou make it; and they shall be for places for the staves to bear it withal. ⁵And thou shalt make the staves of shittim wood, and overlay them with gold. ⁶And thou shalt put it before the vail that is by the ark of the testimony, before the mercy seat that is over the testimony, where I will meet with thee. ⁷And Aaron shall burn thereon sweet incense every morning. When he dresseth the lamps, he shall burn incense upon it. ⁸And when Aaron lighteth the lamps at even, he shall burn incense upon it, a perpetual incense before the Lord throughout your generations. ⁹Ye shall offer no strange incense thereon, nor burnt sacrifice, nor meat offering; neither shall ye pour drink offering thereon. ¹⁰And Aaron shall make an atonement upon the horns of it once in a year with the blood of the sin offering of atonements. Once in the year shall he make atonement upon it throughout your generations. It is most holy unto the Lord.'

¹¹And the Lord spake unto Moses, saying, ¹²'When thou takest the sum of the children of Israel after their number, then shall they give every man a ransom for his soul unto the Lord, when thou numberest them; that there be no

plague among them, when thou numberest them. [13] This they shall give, every one that passeth among them that are numbered, half a shekel after the shekel of the sanctuary (a shekel is twenty gerahs); an half shekel shall be the offering of the Lord. [14] Every one that passeth among them that are numbered, from twenty years old and above, shall give an offering unto the Lord. [15] The rich shall not give more, and the poor shall not give less than half a shekel, when they give an offering unto the Lord, to make an atonement for your souls. [16] And thou shalt take the atonement money of the children of Israel, and shalt appoint it for the service of the tabernacle of the congregation; that it may be a memorial unto the children of Israel before the Lord, to make an atonement for your souls.'

[17] And the Lord spake unto Moses, saying, [18] 'Thou shalt also make a laver of brass, and his foot also of brass, to wash withal; and thou shalt put it between the tabernacle of the congregation and the altar, and thou shalt put water therein. [19] For Aaron and his sons shall wash their hands and their feet thereat. [20] When they go into the tabernacle of the congregation, they shall wash with water, that they die not; or when they come near to the altar to minister, to burn offering made by fire unto the Lord; [21] so they shall wash their hands and their feet, that they die not; and it shall be a statute for ever to them, even to him and to his seed throughout their generations.'

[22] Moreover the Lord spake unto Moses, saying, [23] 'Take thou also unto thee principal spices, of pure myrrh five hundred

shekels, and of sweet cinnamon half so much, even two hundred and fifty shekels, and of sweet calamus two hundred and fifty shekels, 24and of cassia five hundred shekels, after the shekel of the sanctuary, and of oil olive an hin; 25and thou shalt make it an oil of holy ointment, an ointment compound after the art of the apothecary; it shall be an holy anointing oil. 26And thou shalt anoint the tabernacle of the congregation therewith, and the ark of the testimony, 27and the table and all his vessels, and the candlestick and his vessels, and the altar of incense, 28and the altar of burnt offering with all his vessels, and the laver and his foot. 29And thou shalt sanctify them, that they may be most holy; whatsoever toucheth them shall be holy. 30And thou shalt anoint Aaron and his sons, and consecrate them, that they may minister unto me in the priest's office. 31And thou shalt speak unto the children of Israel, saying, "This shall be an holy anointing oil unto me throughout your generations. 32Upon man's flesh shall it not be poured, neither shall ye make any other like it, after the composition of it; it is holy, and it shall be holy unto you. 33Whosoever compoundeth any like it, or whosoever putteth any of it upon a stranger, shall even be cut off from his people."'

34And the Lord said unto Moses, 'Take unto thee sweet spices, stacte, and onycha, and galbanum. These sweet spices with pure frankincense; of each shall there be a like weight, 35and thou shalt make it a perfume, a confection after the art of the apothecary, tempered together, pure and holy. 36And thou shalt beat some of it very small, and put of it before the testimony in the tabernacle of the congregation, where I will meet with thee; it shall be unto you most holy. ³⁷And as for the perfume which thou shalt make, ye shall not make to yourselves according to the composition thereof; it shall be unto thee holy for the Lord. ³⁸ Whosoever shall make like unto that, to smell thereto, shall even be cut off from his people.'

31 And the Lord spake unto Moses, saying, ² 'See, I have called by name Bezaleel the son of Uri, the son of Hur, of the tribe of Judah: ³And I have filled him with the spirit of God, in wisdom, and in understanding, and in knowledge, and in all manner of workmanship, ⁴to devise cunning works, to work in gold, and in silver, and in brass, ⁵ and in cutting of stones, to set them, and in carving of timber, to work in all manner of workmanship. ⁶And I, behold, I have given with him Aholiab, the son of Ahisamach, of the tribe of Dan; and in the hearts of all that are wise hearted I have put wisdom, that they may make all that I have commanded thee: ⁷the tabernacle of the congregation, and the ark of the testimony, and the mercy seat that is thereupon, and all the furniture of the tabernacle, ⁸ and the table and his furniture, and the pure candlestick with all his furniture, and the altar of incense, ⁹ and the altar of burnt offering with all his furniture, and the laver and his foot, ¹⁰ and the cloths of service, and the holy garments for Aaron the priest, and the garments of his sons, to minister in the priest's office, ¹¹and the anointing oil, and sweet incense for the holy place; according to all that I have commanded thee shall they do.'

¹²And the Lord spake unto Moses, saying, ¹³'Speak thou also unto the children of Israel, saying, "Verily my sabbaths ye shall keep, for it is a sign between me and you throughout your generations; that ye may know that I am the Lord that doth sanctify you. ¹⁴Ye shall keep the sabbath therefore; for it is holy unto you; every one that defileth it shall surely be put to death, for whosoever doeth any work therein, that soul shall be cut off from among his people. ¹⁵Six days may work be done; but in the seventh is the sabbath of rest, holy to the Lord; whosoever doeth any work in the sabbath day, he shall surely be put to death. ¹⁶Wherefore the children of Israel shall keep the sabbath, to observe the sabbath throughout their generations, for a perpetual covenant. ¹⁷It is a sign between me and the children of Israel for ever, for in six days the Lord made heaven and earth, and on the seventh day he rested, and was refreshed."'

¹⁸And he gave unto Moses, when he had made an end of communing with him upon mount Sinai, two tables of testimony, tables of stone, written with the finger of God.

32 And when the people saw that Moses delayed to come down out of the mount, the people gathered themselves together unto Aaron, and said unto him, 'Up, make us gods, which shall go before us; for as for this Moses, the man that brought us up out of the land of Egypt, we wot not what is become of him.' ²And Aaron said unto them, 'Break off the golden earrings, which are in the ears of your wives, of your sons, and of your daughters, and bring them unto me.' ³And all the people brake off the golden earrings which were in their ears, and brought them unto Aaron. ⁴And he received them at their hand, and fashioned it with a graving tool, after he had made it a molten calf, and they said, 'These be thy gods, O Israel, which brought thee up out of the land of Egypt.' ⁵And when Aaron saw it, he built an altar before it; and Aaron made proclamation, and said, 'To morrow is a feast to the Lord.' ⁶And they rose up early on the morrow, and offered burnt offerings, and brought peace offerings; and the people sat down to eat and to drink, and rose up to play.

⁷And the Lord said unto Moses, 'Go, get thee down; for thy people, which thou broughtest out of the land of Egypt, have corrupted themselves. ⁸They have turned aside quickly out of the way which I commanded them: they have made them a molten calf, and have worshipped it, and have sacrificed thereunto, and said, "These be thy gods, O Israel, which have brought thee up out of the land of Egypt."' ⁹And the Lord said unto Moses, 'I have seen this people, and, behold, it is a stiffnecked people. ¹⁰Now therefore let me alone, that my wrath may wax hot against them, and that I may consume them, and I will make of thee a great nation.' ¹¹And Moses besought the Lord his God, and said, 'Lord, why doth thy wrath wax hot against thy people, which thou hast brought forth out of the land of Egypt with great power, and with a mighty hand? ¹²Wherefore should the Egyptians speak, and say, "For mischief did he bring them out, to slay them in the mountains, and to consume them from the face of the earth?" Turn from thy fierce wrath, and repent of this evil against

thy people. ¹³Remember Abraham, Isaac, and Israel, thy servants, to whom thou swarest by thine own self, and saidst unto them, "I will multiply your seed as the stars of heaven, and all this land that I have spoken of will I give unto your seed, and they shall inherit it for ever."' ¹⁴And the Lord repented of the evil which he thought to do unto his people.

¹⁵And Moses turned, and went down from the mount, and the two tables of the testimony were in his hand. The tables were written on both their sides; on the one side and on the other were they written. ¹⁶And the tables were the work of God, and the writing was the writing of God, graven upon the tables. ¹⁷And when Joshua heard the noise of the people as they shouted, he said unto Moses, 'There is a noise of war in the camp.' ¹⁸And he said, 'It is not the voice of them that shout for mastery, neither is it the voice of them that cry for being overcome, but the noise of them that sing do I hear.'

¹⁹And it came to pass, as soon as he came nigh unto the camp, that he saw the calf, and the dancing; and Moses' anger waxed hot, and he cast the tables out of his hands, and brake them beneath the mount. ²⁰And he took the calf which they had made, and burnt it in the fire, and ground it to powder, and strawed it upon the water, and made the children of Israel drink of it. ²¹And Moses said unto Aaron, 'What did this people unto thee, that thou hast brought so great a sin upon them?' ²²And Aaron said, 'Let not the anger of my lord wax hot; thou knowest the people, that they are set on mischief. ²³For they said unto me, "Make us gods, which shall go before us, for as for this Moses, the man that brought us

up out of the land of Egypt, we wot not what is become of him." ²⁴And I said unto them, "Whosoever hath any gold, let them break it off." So they gave it me; then I cast it into the fire, and there came out this calf.'

²⁵And when Moses saw that the people were naked (for Aaron had made them naked unto their shame among their enemies), ²⁶then Moses stood in the gate of the camp, and said, 'Who is on the Lord's side? Let him come unto me.' And all the sons of Levi gathered themselves together unto him. ²⁷And he said unto them, 'Thus saith the Lord God of Israel, "Put every man his sword by his side, and go in and out from gate to gate throughout the camp, and slay every man his brother, and every man his companion, and every man his neighbour."' ²⁸And the children of Levi did according to the word of Moses, and there fell of the people that day about three thousand men. ²⁹For Moses had said, 'Consecrate yourselves today to the Lord, even every man upon his son, and upon his brother, that he may bestow upon you a blessing this day.'

³⁰And it came to pass on the morrow, that Moses said unto the people, 'Ye have sinned a great sin, and now I will go up unto the Lord; peradventure I shall make an atonement for your sin.' ³¹And Moses returned unto the Lord, and said, 'Oh, this people have sinned a great sin, and have made them gods of gold. ³²Yet now, if thou wilt forgive their sin—; and if not, blot me, I pray thee, out of thy book which thou hast written.' ³³And the Lord said unto Moses, 'Whosoever hath sinned against me, him will I blot out of my book.

[34] Therefore now go, lead the people unto the place of which I have spoken unto thee. Behold, mine Angel shall go before thee; nevertheless in the day when I visit I will visit their sin upon them.' [35] And the Lord plagued the people, because they made the calf, which Aaron made.

33 And the Lord said unto Moses, 'Depart, and go up hence, thou and the people which thou hast brought up out of the land of Egypt, unto the land which I sware unto Abraham, to Isaac, and to Jacob, saying, "Unto thy seed will I give it." [2] And I will send an angel before thee; and I will drive out the Canaanite, the Amorite, and the Hittite, and the Perizzite, the Hivite, and the Jebusite, [3] unto a land flowing with milk and honey, for I will not go up in the midst of thee; for thou art a stiffnecked people, lest I consume thee in the way.'

[4] And when the people heard these evil tidings, they mourned, and no man did put on him his ornaments. [5] For the Lord had said unto Moses, 'Say unto the children of Israel, "Ye are a stiffnecked people. I will come up into the midst of thee in a moment, and consume thee; therefore now put off thy ornaments from thee, that I may know what to do unto thee."' [6] And the children of Israel stripped themselves of their ornaments by the mount Horeb. [7] And Moses took the tabernacle, and pitched it without the camp, afar off from the camp, and called it the Tabernacle of the congregation. And it came to pass, that every one which sought the Lord went out unto the tabernacle of the congregation, which was without the camp. [8] And it came to pass, when Moses went out

unto the tabernacle, that all the people rose up, and stood every man at his tent door, and looked after Moses, until he was gone into the tabernacle. ⁹And it came to pass, as Moses entered into the tabernacle, the cloudy pillar descended, and stood at the door of the tabernacle, and the Lord talked with Moses. ¹⁰And all the people saw the cloudy pillar stand at the tabernacle door, and all the people rose up and worshipped, every man in his tent door. ¹¹And the Lord spake unto Moses face to face, as a man speaketh unto his friend. And he turned again into the camp, but his servant Joshua, the son of Nun, a young man, departed not out of the tabernacle.

¹²And Moses said unto the Lord, 'See, thou sayest unto me, "Bring up this people,' and thou hast not let me know whom thou wilt send with me. Yet thou hast said, "I know thee by name, and thou hast also found grace in my sight." ¹³Now therefore, I pray thee, if I have found grace in thy sight, shew me now thy way, that I may know thee, that I may find grace in thy sight; and consider that this nation is thy people.' ¹⁴And he said, 'My presence shall go with thee, and I will give thee rest.' ¹⁵And he said unto him, 'If thy presence go not with me, carry us not up hence. ¹⁶For wherein shall it be known here that I and thy people have found grace in thy sight? Is it not in that thou goest with us? So shall we be separated, I and thy people, from all the people that are upon the face of the earth.' ¹⁷And the Lord said unto Moses, 'I will do this thing also that thou hast spoken, for thou hast found grace in my sight, and I know thee by name.' ¹⁸And he said, 'I beseech thee, shew me thy glory.' ¹⁹And he said, 'I will make

all my goodness pass before thee, and I will proclaim the name of the Lord before thee; and will be gracious to whom I will be gracious, and will shew mercy on whom I will shew mercy.' ²⁰And he said, 'Thou canst not see my face, for there shall no man see me, and live.' ²¹And the Lord said, 'Behold, there is a place by me, and thou shalt stand upon a rock. ²²And it shall come to pass, while my glory passeth by, that I will put thee in a clift of the rock, and will cover thee with my hand while I pass by. ²³And I will take away mine hand, and thou shalt see my back parts, but my face shall not be seen.'

34 And the Lord said unto Moses, 'Hew thee two tables of stone like unto the first, and I will write upon these tables the words that were in the first tables, which thou brakest. ²And be ready in the morning, and come up in the morning unto mount Sinai, and present thyself there to me in the top of the mount. ³And no man shall come up with thee, neither let any man be seen throughout all the mount; neither let the flocks nor herds feed before that mount.'

⁴And he hewed two tables of stone like unto the first; and Moses rose up early in the morning, and went up unto mount Sinai, as the Lord had commanded him, and took in his hand the two tables of stone. ⁵And the Lord descended in the cloud, and stood with him there, and proclaimed the name of the Lord. ⁶And the Lord passed by before him, and proclaimed, 'The Lord, The Lord God, merciful and gracious, long-suffering, and abundant in goodness and truth, ⁷ keeping mercy for thousands, forgiving iniquity and transgression and sin,

and that will by no means clear the guilty, visiting the iniquity of the fathers upon the children, and upon the children's children, unto the third and to the fourth generation.' ⁸And Moses made haste, and bowed his head toward the earth, and worshipped. ⁹And he said, 'If now I have found grace in thy sight, O Lord, let my Lord, I pray thee, go among us; for it is a stiffnecked people; and pardon our iniquity and our sin, and take us for thine inheritance.'

¹⁰And he said, 'Behold, I make a covenant; before all thy people I will do marvels, such as have not been done in all the earth, nor in any nation; and all the people among which thou art shall see the work of the Lord, for it is a terrible thing that I will do with thee. ¹¹Observe thou that which I command thee this day; behold, I drive out before thee the Amorite, and the Canaanite, and the Hittite, and the Perizzite, and the Hivite, and the Jebusite. ¹²Take heed to thyself, lest thou make a covenant with the inhabitants of the land whither thou goest, lest it be for a snare in the midst of thee. ¹³But ye shall destroy their altars, break their images, and cut down their groves, ¹⁴for thou shalt worship no other god, for the Lord, whose name is Jealous, is a jealous God, ¹⁵lest thou make a covenant with the inhabitants of the land, and they go a whoring after their gods, and do sacrifice unto their gods, and one call thee, and thou eat of his sacrifice; ¹⁶and thou take of their daughters unto thy sons, and their daughters go a whoring after their gods, and make thy sons go a whoring after their gods. ¹⁷Thou shalt make thee no molten gods.

¹⁸'The feast of unleavened bread shalt thou keep. Seven

days thou shalt eat unleavened bread, as I commanded thee, in the time of the month Abib, for in the month Abib thou camest out from Egypt. ¹⁹All that openeth the matrix is mine; and every firstling among thy cattle, whether ox or sheep, that is male. ²⁰But the firstling of an ass thou shalt redeem with a lamb, and if thou redeem him not, then shalt thou break his neck. All the firstborn of thy sons thou shalt redeem. And none shall appear before me empty.

²¹'Six days thou shalt work, but on the seventh day thou shalt rest; in earing time and in harvest thou shalt rest.

²²'And thou shalt observe the feast of weeks, of the first-fruits of wheat harvest, and the feast of ingathering at the year's end.

²³'Thrice in the year shall all your men children appear before the Lord God, the God of Israel. ²⁴For I will cast out the nations before thee, and enlarge thy borders; neither shall any man desire thy land, when thou shalt go up to appear before the Lord thy God thrice in the year. ²⁵Thou shalt not offer the blood of my sacrifice with leaven; neither shall the sacrifice of the feast of the passover be left unto the morning. ²⁶The first of the firstfruits of thy land thou shalt bring unto the house of the Lord thy God. Thou shalt not seethe a kid in his mother's milk.' ²⁷And the Lord said unto Moses, 'Write thou these words, for after the tenor of these words I have made a covenant with thee and with Israel.' ²⁸And he was there with the Lord forty days and forty nights; he did neither eat bread, nor drink water. And he wrote upon the tables the words of the covenant, the ten commandments.

²⁹And it came to pass, when Moses came down from mount Sinai with the two tables of testimony in Moses' hand, when he came down from the mount, that Moses wist not that the skin of his face shone while he talked with him. ³⁰And when Aaron and all the children of Israel saw Moses, behold, the skin of his face shone; and they were afraid to come nigh him. ³¹And Moses called unto them; and Aaron and all the rulers of the congregation returned unto him; and Moses talked with them. ³²And afterward all the children of Israel came nigh; and he gave them in commandment all that the Lord had spoken with him in mount Sinai. ³³And till Moses had done speaking with them, he put a vail on his face. ³⁴ But when Moses went in before the Lord to speak with him, he took the vail off, until he came out. And he came out, and spake unto the children of Israel that which he was commanded. ³⁵And the children of Israel saw the face of Moses, that the skin of Moses' face shone, and Moses put the vail upon his face again, until he went in to speak with him.

35 And Moses gathered all the congregation of the children of Israel together, and said unto them, 'These are the words which the Lord hath commanded, that ye should do them. ²"Six days shall work be done, but on the seventh day there shall be to you an holy day, a sabbath of rest to the Lord; whosoever doeth work therein shall be put to death. ³Ye shall kindle no fire throughout your habitations upon the sabbath day."'

⁴And Moses spake unto all the congregation of the children

of Israel, saying, 'This is the thing which the Lord commanded, saying, ⁵ "Take ye from among you an offering unto the Lord; whosoever is of a willing heart, let him bring it, an offering of the Lord; gold, and silver, and brass, ⁶ and blue, and purple, and scarlet, and fine linen, and goats' hair, ⁷ and rams' skins dyed red, and badgers' skins, and shittim wood, ⁸ and oil for the light, and spices for anointing oil, and for the sweet incense, ⁹ and onyx stones, and stones to be set for the ephod, and for the breastplate. ¹⁰ And every wise hearted among you shall come, and make all that the Lord hath commanded: ¹¹ the tabernacle, his tent, and his covering, his taches, and his boards, his bars, his pillars, and his sockets, ¹² the ark, and the staves thereof, with the mercy seat, and the vail of the covering, ¹³ the table, and his staves, and all his vessels, and the shewbread, ¹⁴ the candlestick also for the light, and his furniture, and his lamps, with the oil for the light, ¹⁵ and the incense altar, and his staves, and the anointing oil, and the sweet incense, and the hanging for the door at the entering in of the tabernacle, ¹⁶ the altar of burnt offering, with his brasen grate, his staves, and all his vessels, the laver and his foot, ¹⁷ the hangings of the court, his pillars, and their sockets, and the hanging for the door of the court, ¹⁸ the pins of the tabernacle, and the pins of the court, and their cords, ¹⁹ the cloths of service, to do service in the holy place, the holy garments for Aaron the priest, and the garments of his sons, to minister in the priest's office."'

²⁰ And all the congregation of the children of Israel departed from the presence of Moses. ²¹ And they came, every one

whose heart stirred him up, and every one whom his spirit made willing, and they brought the Lord's offering to the work of the tabernacle of the congregation, and for all his service, and for the holy garments. ²²And they came, both men and women, as many as were willing hearted, and brought bracelets, and earrings, and rings, and tablets, all jewels of gold; and every man that offered an offering of gold unto the Lord. ²³And every man, with whom was found blue, and purple, and scarlet, and fine linen, and goats' hair, and red skins of rams, and badgers' skins, brought them. ²⁴Every one that did offer an offering of silver and brass brought the Lord's offering; and every man, with whom was found shittim wood for any work of the service, brought it. ²⁵And all the women that were wise hearted did spin with their hands, and brought that which they had spun, both of blue, and of purple, and of scarlet, and of fine linen. ²⁶And all the women whose heart stirred them up in wisdom spun goats' hair. ²⁷And the rulers brought onyx stones, and stones to be set, for the ephod, and for the breastplate; ²⁸and spice, and oil for the light, and for the anointing oil, and for the sweet incense. ²⁹The children of Israel brought a willing offering unto the Lord, every man and woman, whose heart made them willing to bring for all manner of work, which the Lord had commanded to be made by the hand of Moses.

³⁰And Moses said unto the children of Israel, 'See, the Lord hath called by name Bezaleel the son of Uri, the son of Hur, of the tribe of Judah; ³¹and he hath filled him with the spirit of God, in wisdom, in understanding, and in knowledge,

and in all manner of workmanship; ³²and to devise curious works, to work in gold, and in silver, and in brass, ³³and in the cutting of stones, to set them, and in carving of wood, to make any manner of cunning work. ³⁴And he hath put in his heart that he may teach, both he, and Aholiab, the son of Ahisamach, of the tribe of Dan. ³⁵Them hath he filled with wisdom of heart, to work all manner of work, of the engraver, and of the cunning workman, and of the embroiderer, in blue, and in purple, in scarlet, and in fine linen, and of the weaver, even of them that do any work, and of those that devise cunning work.'

36 Then wrought Bezaleel and Aholiab, and every wise hearted man, in whom the Lord put wisdom and understanding to know how to work all manner of work for the service of the sanctuary, according to all that the Lord had commanded. ²And Moses called Bezaleel and Aholiab, and every wise hearted man, in whose heart the Lord had put wisdom, even every one whose heart stirred him up to come unto the work to do it; ³and they received of Moses all the offering, which the children of Israel had brought for the work of the service of the sanctuary, to make it withal. And they brought yet unto him free offerings every morning. ⁴And all the wise men, that wrought all the work of the sanctuary, came every man from his work which they made; ⁵and they spake unto Moses, saying, 'The people bring much more than enough for the service of the work, which the Lord commanded to make.' ⁶And Moses gave commandment,

and they caused it to be proclaimed throughout the camp, saying, 'Let neither man nor woman make any more work for the offering of the sanctuary.' So the people were restrained from bringing. ⁷ For the stuff they had was sufficient for all the work to make it, and too much.

⁸And every wise hearted man among them that wrought the work of the tabernacle made ten curtains of fine twined linen, and blue, and purple, and scarlet; with cherubims of cunning work made he them. ⁹ The length of one curtain was twenty and eight cubits, and the breadth of one curtain four cubits; the curtains were all of one size. ¹⁰And he coupled the five curtains one unto another, and the other five curtains he coupled one unto another. ¹¹And he made loops of blue on the edge of one curtain from the selvedge in the coupling; likewise he made in the uttermost side of another curtain, in the coupling of the second. ¹² Fifty loops made he in one curtain, and fifty loops made he in the edge of the curtain which was in the coupling of the second; the loops held one curtain to another. ¹³And he made fifty taches of gold, and coupled the curtains one unto another with the taches; so it became one tabernacle.

¹⁴And he made curtains of goats' hair for the tent over the tabernacle; eleven curtains he made them. ¹⁵ The length of one curtain was thirty cubits, and four cubits was the breadth of one curtain; the eleven curtains were of one size. ¹⁶And he coupled five curtains by themselves, and six curtains by themselves. ¹⁷And he made fifty loops upon the uttermost edge of the curtain in the coupling, and fifty loops made he upon the

edge of the curtain which coupleth the second. [18]And he made fifty taches of brass to couple the tent together, that it might be one. [19]And he made a covering for the tent of rams' skins dyed red, and a covering of badgers' skins above that.

[20]And he made boards for the tabernacle of shittim wood, standing up. [21]The length of a board was ten cubits, and the breadth of a board one cubit and a half. [22]One board had two tenons, equally distant one from another; thus did he make for all the boards of the tabernacle. [23]And he made boards for the tabernacle; twenty boards for the south side southward. [24]And forty sockets of silver he made under the twenty boards; two sockets under one board for his two tenons, and two sockets under another board for his two tenons. [25]And for the other side of the tabernacle, which is toward the north corner, he made twenty boards, [26]and their forty sockets of silver; two sockets under one board, and two sockets under another board. [27]And for the sides of the tabernacle westward he made six boards. [28]And two boards made he for the corners of the tabernacle in the two sides. [29]And they were coupled beneath, and coupled together at the head thereof, to one ring; thus he did to both of them in both the corners. [30]And there were eight boards; and their sockets were sixteen sockets of silver, under every board two sockets.

[31]And he made bars of shittim wood; five for the boards of the one side of the tabernacle, [32]and five bars for the boards of the other side of the tabernacle, and five bars for the boards of the tabernacle for the sides westward. [33]And he made the middle bar to shoot through the boards from the

one end to the other. ³⁴And he overlaid the boards with gold, and made their rings of gold to be places for the bars, and overlaid the bars with gold.

³⁵And he made a vail of blue, and purple, and scarlet, and fine twined linen; with cherubims made he it of cunning work. ³⁶And he made thereunto four pillars of shittim wood, and overlaid them with gold; their hooks were of gold; and he cast for them four sockets of silver.

³⁷And he made an hanging for the tabernacle door of blue, and purple, and scarlet, and fine twined linen, of needle-work; ³⁸and the five pillars of it with their hooks; and he overlaid their chapiters and their fillets with gold; but their five sockets were of brass.

37 And Bezaleel made the ark of shittim wood; two cubits and a half was the length of it, and a cubit and a half the breadth of it, and a cubit and a half the height of it; ²and he overlaid it with pure gold within and without, and made a crown of gold to it round about. ³And he cast for it four rings of gold, to be set by the four corners of it; even two rings upon the one side of it, and two rings upon the other side of it. ⁴And he made staves of shittim wood, and overlaid them with gold. ⁵And he put the staves into the rings by the sides of the ark, to bear the ark.

⁶And he made the mercy seat of pure gold; two cubits and a half was the length thereof, and one cubit and a half the breadth thereof. ⁷And he made two cherubims of gold, beaten out of one piece made he them, on the two ends of

the mercy seat; 8 one cherub on the end on this side, and another cherub on the other end on that side; out of the mercy seat made he the cherubims on the two ends thereof. 9 And the cherubims spread out their wings on high, and covered with their wings over the mercy seat, with their faces one to another; even to the mercy seatward were the faces of the cherubims.

10 And he made the table of shittim wood; two cubits was the length thereof, and a cubit the breadth thereof, and a cubit and a half the height thereof. 11 And he overlaid it with pure gold, and made thereunto a crown of gold round about. 12 Also he made thereunto a border of an handbreadth round about; and made a crown of gold for the border thereof round about. 13 And he cast for it four rings of gold, and put the rings upon the four corners that were in the four feet thereof. 14 Over against the border were the rings, the places for the staves to bear the table. 15 And he made the staves of shittim wood, and overlaid them with gold, to bear the table. 16 And he made the vessels which were upon the table, his dishes, and his spoons, and his bowls, and his covers to cover withal, of pure gold.

17 And he made the candlestick of pure gold; of beaten work made he the candlestick; his shaft, and his branch, his bowls, his knops, and his flowers, were of the same; 18 and six branches going out of the sides thereof; three branches of the candlestick out of the one side thereof, and three branches of the candlestick out of the other side thereof; 19 three bowls made after the fashion of almonds in one branch, a knop and

a flower; and three bowls made like almonds in another branch, a knop and a flower; so throughout the six branches going out of the candlestick. ²⁰And in the candlestick were four bowls made like almonds, his knops, and his flowers; ²¹and a knop under two branches of the same, and a knop under two branches of the same, and a knop under two branches of the same, according to the six branches going out of it. ²²Their knops and their branches were of the same; all of it was one beaten work of pure gold. ²³And he made his seven lamps, and his snuffers, and his snuffdishes, of pure gold. ²⁴Of a talent of pure gold made he it, and all the vessels thereof.

²⁵And he made the incense altar of shittim wood; the length of it was a cubit, and the breadth of it a cubit; it was foursquare; and two cubits was the height of it; the horns thereof were of the same. ²⁶And he overlaid it with pure gold, both the top of it, and the sides thereof round about, and the horns of it; also he made unto it a crown of gold round about. ²⁷And he made two rings of gold for it under the crown thereof, by the two corners of it, upon the two sides thereof, to be places for the staves to bear it withal. ²⁸And he made the staves of shittim wood, and overlaid them with gold.

²⁹And he made the holy anointing oil, and the pure incense of sweet spices, according to the work of the apothecary.

38 And he made the altar of burnt offering of shittim wood; five cubits was the length thereof, and five cubits the breadth thereof; it was foursquare; and three cubits the height thereof. ²And he made the horns thereof on the

four corners of it; the horns thereof were of the same; and he overlaid it with brass. ³And he made all the vessels of the altar, the pots, and the shovels, and the basons, and the flesh-hooks, and the firepans; all the vessels thereof made he of brass. ⁴And he made for the altar a brasen grate of network under the compass thereof beneath unto the midst of it. ⁵And he cast four rings for the four ends of the grate of brass, to be places for the staves. ⁶And he made the staves of shittim wood, and overlaid them with brass. ⁷And he put the staves into the rings on the sides of the altar, to bear it withal; he made the altar hollow with boards.

⁸And he made the laver of brass, and the foot of it of brass, of the looking-glasses of the women assembling, which assembled at the door of the tabernacle of the congregation.

⁹And he made the court; on the south side southward the hangings of the court were of fine twined linen, an hundred cubits; ¹⁰ their pillars were twenty, and their brasen sockets twenty; the hooks of the pillars and their fillets were of silver. ¹¹And for the north side the hangings were an hundred cubits, their pillars were twenty, and their sockets of brass twenty; the hooks of the pillars and their fillets of silver. ¹²And for the west side were hangings of fifty cubits, their pillars ten, and their sockets ten; the hooks of the pillars and their fillets of silver. ¹³And for the east side eastward fifty cubits. ¹⁴The hangings of the one side of the gate were fifteen cubits; their pillars three, and their sockets three. ¹⁵And for the other side of the court gate, on this hand and that hand, were hangings of fifteen cubits; their pillars three, and their

sockets three. ¹⁶All the hangings of the court round about were of fine twined linen. ¹⁷And the sockets for the pillars were of brass; the hooks of the pillars and their fillets of silver; and the overlaying of their chapiters of silver; and all the pillars of the court were filleted with silver. ¹⁸And the hanging for the gate of the court was needlework, of blue, and purple, and scarlet, and fine twined linen; and twenty cubits was the length, and the height in the breadth was five cubits, answerable to the hangings of the court. ¹⁹And their pillars were four, and their sockets of brass four; their hooks of silver, and the overlaying of their chapiters and their fillets of silver. ²⁰And all the pins of the tabernacle, and of the court round about, were of brass.

²¹This is the sum of the tabernacle, even of the tabernacle of testimony, as it was counted, according to the commandment of Moses, for the service of the Levites, by the hand of Ithamar, son to Aaron the priest. ²²And Bezaleel the son of Uri, the son of Hur, of the tribe of Judah, made all that the Lord commanded Moses. ²³And with him was Aholiab, son of Ahisamach, of the tribe of Dan, an engraver, and a cunning workman, and an embroiderer in blue, and in purple, and in scarlet, and fine linen. ²⁴All the gold that was occupied for the work in all the work of the holy place, even the gold of the offering, was twenty and nine talents, and seven hundred and thirty shekels, after the shekel of the sanctuary. ²⁵And the silver of them that were numbered of the congregation was an hundred talents, and a thousand seven hundred and threescore and fifteen shekels, after the shekel of

the sanctuary: ²⁶ a bekah for every man, that is, half a shekel, after the shekel of the sanctuary, for every one that went to be numbered, from twenty years old and upward, for six hundred thousand and three thousand and five hundred and fifty men. ²⁷ And of the hundred talents of silver were cast the sockets of the sanctuary, and the sockets of the vail; an hundred sockets of the hundred talents, a talent for a socket. ²⁸ And of the thousand seven hundred seventy and five shekels he made hooks for the pillars, and overlaid their chapiters, and filleted them. ²⁹ And the brass of the offering was seventy talents, and two thousand and four hundred shekels. ³⁰ And therewith he made the sockets to the door of the tabernacle of the congregation, and the brasen altar, and the brasen grate for it, and all the vessels of the altar, ³¹ and the sockets of the court round about, and the sockets of the court gate, and all the pins of the tabernacle, and all the pins of the court round about.

39 And of the blue, and purple, and scarlet, they made cloths of service, to do service in the holy place, and made the holy garments for Aaron; as the Lord commanded Moses. ²And he made the ephod of gold, blue, and purple, and scarlet, and fine twined linen. ³And they did beat the gold into thin plates, and cut it into wires, to work it in the blue, and in the purple, and in the scarlet, and in the fine linen, with cunning work. ⁴They made shoulderpieces for it, to couple it together; by the two edges was it coupled together. ⁵And the curious girdle of his ephod, that was upon it, was

of the same, according to the work thereof; of gold, blue, and purple, and scarlet, and fine twined linen; as the Lord commanded Moses.

⁶And they wrought onyx stones inclosed in ouches of gold, graven, as signets are graven, with the names of the children of Israel. ⁷And he put them on the shoulders of the ephod, that they should be stones for a memorial to the children of Israel, as the Lord commanded Moses.

⁸And he made the breastplate of cunning work, like the work of the ephod; of gold, blue, and purple, and scarlet, and fine twined linen. ⁹It was foursquare; they made the breastplate double; a span was the length thereof, and a span the breadth thereof, being doubled. ¹⁰And they set in it four rows of stones; the first row was a sardius, a topaz, and a carbuncle; this was the first row. ¹¹And the second row, an emerald, a sapphire, and a diamond. ¹²And the third row, a ligure, an agate, and an amethyst. ¹³And the fourth row, a beryl, an onyx, and a jasper; they were inclosed in ouches of gold in their inclosings. ¹⁴And the stones were according to the names of the children of Israel, twelve, according to their names, like the engravings of a signet, every one with his name, according to the twelve tribes. ¹⁵And they made upon the breastplate chains at the ends, of wreathen work of pure gold. ¹⁶And they made two ouches of gold, and two gold rings; and put the two rings in the two ends of the breastplate. ¹⁷And they put the two wreathen chains of gold in the two rings on the ends of the breastplate. ¹⁸And the two ends of the two wreathen chains they fastened in the two ouches, and put them

on the shoulderpieces of the ephod, before it. ¹⁹And they made two rings of gold, and put them on the two ends of the breastplate, upon the border of it, which was on the side of the ephod inward. ²⁰And they made two other golden rings, and put them on the two sides of the ephod underneath, toward the forepart of it, over against the other coupling thereof, above the curious girdle of the ephod. ²¹And they did bind the breastplate by his rings unto the rings of the ephod with a lace of blue, that it might be above the curious girdle of the ephod, and that the breastplate might not be loosed from the ephod; as the Lord commanded Moses.

²²And he made the robe of the ephod of woven work, all of blue. ²³And there was an hole in the midst of the robe, as the hole of an habergeon, with a band round about the hole, that it should not rend. ²⁴And they made upon the hems of the robe pomegranates of blue, and purple, and scarlet, and twined linen. ²⁵And they made bells of pure gold, and put the bells between the pomegranates upon the hem of the robe, round about between the pomegranates: ²⁶a bell and a pomegranate, a bell and a pomegranate, round about the hem of the robe to minister in; as the Lord commanded Moses.

²⁷And they made coats of fine linen of woven work for Aaron, and for his sons, ²⁸and a mitre of fine linen, and goodly bonnets of fine linen, and linen breeches of fine twined linen, ²⁹and a girdle of fine twined linen, and blue, and purple, and scarlet, of needlework, as the Lord commanded Moses.

³⁰And they made the plate of the holy crown of pure gold, and wrote upon it a writing, like to the engravings of a

signet, 'Holiness to the Lord.' ³¹And they tied unto it a lace of blue, to fasten it on high upon the mitre; as the Lord commanded Moses.

³² Thus was all the work of the tabernacle of the tent of the congregation finished; and the children of Israel did according to all that the Lord commanded Moses, so did they.

³³And they brought the tabernacle unto Moses, the tent, and all his furniture, his taches, his boards, his bars, and his pillars, and his sockets, ³⁴ and the covering of rams' skins dyed red, and the covering of badgers' skins, and the vail of the covering, ³⁵ the ark of the testimony, and the staves thereof, and the mercy seat, ³⁶ the table, and all the vessels thereof, and the shewbread, ³⁷ the pure candlestick, with the lamps thereof, even with the lamps to be set in order, and all the vessels thereof, and the oil for light, ³⁸ and the golden altar, and the anointing oil, and the sweet incense, and the hanging for the tabernacle door, ³⁹ the brasen altar, and his grate of brass, his staves, and all his vessels, the laver and his foot, ⁴⁰ the hangings of the court, his pillars, and his sockets, and the hanging for the court gate, his cords, and his pins, and all the vessels of the service of the tabernacle, for the tent of the congregation, ⁴¹ the cloths of service to do service in the holy place, and the holy garments for Aaron the priest, and his sons' garments, to minister in the priest's office. ⁴²According to all that the Lord commanded Moses, so the children of Israel made all the work. ⁴³And Moses did look upon all the work, and, behold, they had done it as the Lord had commanded, even so had they done it; and Moses blessed them.

40 And the Lord spake unto Moses, saying, ² 'On the first day of the first month shalt thou set up the tabernacle of the tent of the congregation. ³And thou shalt put therein the ark of the testimony, and cover the ark with the vail. ⁴And thou shalt bring in the table, and set in order the things that are to be set in order upon it; and thou shalt bring in the candlestick, and light the lamps thereof. ⁵And thou shalt set the altar of gold for the incense before the ark of the testimony, and put the hanging of the door to the tabernacle. ⁶And thou shalt set the altar of the burnt offering before the door of the tabernacle of the tent of the congregation. ⁷And thou shalt set the laver between the tent of the congregation and the altar, and shalt put water therein. ⁸And thou shalt set up the court round about, and hang up the hanging at the court gate. ⁹And thou shalt take the anointing oil, and anoint the tabernacle, and all that is therein, and shalt hallow it, and all the vessels thereof; and it shall be holy. ¹⁰And thou shalt anoint the altar of the burnt offering, and all his vessels, and sanctify the altar; and it shall be an altar most holy. ¹¹And thou shalt anoint the laver and his foot, and sanctify it. ¹²And thou shalt bring Aaron and his sons unto the door of the tabernacle of the congregation, and wash them with water. ¹³And thou shalt put upon Aaron the holy garments, and anoint him, and sanctify him, that he may minister unto me in the priest's office. ¹⁴And thou shalt bring his sons, and clothe them with coats; ¹⁵and thou shalt anoint them, as thou didst anoint their father, that they may minister unto me in the priest's office: for their anointing shall surely be an everlasting priesthood throughout their generations.' ¹⁶ Thus did Moses; according to all that the Lord commanded him, so did he.

¹⁷And it came to pass in the first month in the second year, on the first day of the month, that the tabernacle was reared up. ¹⁸And Moses reared up the tabernacle, and fastened his sockets, and set up the boards thereof, and put in the bars thereof, and reared up his pillars. ¹⁹And he spread abroad the tent over the tabernacle, and put the covering of the tent above upon it, as the Lord commanded Moses.

²⁰And he took and put the testimony into the ark, and set the staves on the ark, and put the mercy seat above upon the ark. ²¹And he brought the ark into the tabernacle, and set up the vail of the covering, and covered the ark of the testimony, as the Lord commanded Moses.

²²And he put the table in the tent of the congregation, upon the side of the tabernacle northward, without the vail. ²³And he set the bread in order upon it before the Lord, as the Lord had commanded Moses.

²⁴And he put the candlestick in the tent of the congregation, over against the table, on the side of the tabernacle southward. ²⁵And he lighted the lamps before the Lord, as the Lord commanded Moses.

²⁶And he put the golden altar in the tent of the congregation before the vail; ²⁷and he burnt sweet incense thereon, as the Lord commanded Moses.

²⁸And he set up the hanging at the door of the tabernacle. ²⁹And he put the altar of burnt offering by the door of the

tabernacle of the tent of the congregation, and offered upon it the burnt offering and the meat offering, as the Lord commanded Moses.

[30]And he set the laver between the tent of the congregation and the altar, and put water there, to wash withal. [31]And Moses and Aaron and his sons washed their hands and their feet thereat. [32] When they went into the tent of the congregation, and when they came near unto the altar, they washed, as the Lord commanded Moses. [33]And he reared up the court round about the tabernacle and the altar, and set up the hanging of the court gate. So Moses finished the work.

[34] Then a cloud covered the tent of the congregation, and the glory of the Lord filled the tabernacle. [35]And Moses was not able to enter into the tent of the congregation, because the cloud abode thereon, and the glory of the Lord filled the tabernacle. [36]And when the cloud was taken up from over the tabernacle, the children of Israel went onward in all their journeys; [37] but if the cloud were not taken up, then they journeyed not till the day that it was taken up. [38] For the cloud of the Lord was upon the tabernacle by day, and fire was on it by night, in the sight of all the house of Israel, throughout all their journeys.

titles in the series